Above the Ashes

A memoir by Kevin P. Conley Jr.

Edited by: Elizabeth Ridley

Foreword

by Ben Strahan, California Hotshot Superintendent:

As I write the foreword to this book, I still have never met Kevin. In fact, the first time we talked was when he asked if I would write the foreword to his book. My initial feeling was one of excitement and caution. You see, I've heard about Kevin. He's the dude that rode his bike across the States with his pup, raising money for the Wildland Firefighter Foundation, a foundation helping Wildland Firefighters and their families when in need. If I'm speaking truthfully, this was my extent of knowing who Kevin is and his story. So, it was a bit interesting to see how I fit into this picture.

As our first conversation went on, Kevin described his journey across America, the money he raised, but more importantly, what drove him to go on such a journey. He briefly presented his story and asked if I would check out the podcast episodes he did with *The Anchor Point Podcast*. I agreed to both, the foreword and the research I needed to do to understand Kevin better. After my research into who Kevin is and what he has done, I became fueled by this need to talk with him about his story and had an overwhelming feeling of connection to him.

You see, what I came to understand is that Kevin's story, his life, and his path to personal growth, were powerful. More importantly, the story he was telling was my story; it was our story. There are many different parts about his journey that are uniquely his, but the cause and effect are the same for most of us. Stress leads to attachments, then leads to suffering, and as suffering grows, we will reach a decision point; continue to let the suffering grow, or display courage and heal. As wildland firefighters we are constantly exposed to risk and stress, and many of us lack the tools or know-how when it comes to healing.

What you will find in this book is what I found, a well-written story of Kevin's journey that relates to our story through shared perspective. It's this shared perspective that he gifts us so we can see our existence and experiences within his. Kevin beautifully takes us on a journey through personal suffering, then learning, and finally letting go and growth.

One conversation we had was about how being vulnerable is the first step to living your truth; this book Kevin has written, is this process. It puts out there his vulnerabilities then builds to his truth, the truth we all seek, the truth that it is living that we should value most. This story, this journey, is told from Kevin's perspective, and one that has many threads as a Wildland Firefighter. But know this, Kevin, more than anything, provides human perspective. Each lesson provided has the ability to connect us all and provide the fire we may need to endure our personal suffering. Let Kevin's courage provide you the courage you need to find your truth.

Thank you, Kevin, for this beautiful opportunity to be a part of your life story and bringing many people from a place of knowing to understanding. I honor you, Brother

I dedicate this book to all the men and women who risk their lives fighting wildfires.

For the past, present, and future wildland firefighters, this one's for you.

It's with great honor I can say you're my brothers and sisters.

Thank you for being there for me; I will always be there for you.

Rest In Peace to the brave, honorable Wildland Firefighters who have lost their lives in this job.

One day, we will tie in again.

PROLOGUE

Into the darkness I was thrown. It was as if I were a glass ball, delicate and way too fragile for my surroundings, clicking and crashing as I went tumbling down a mountain. For some reason, through the violent descent, I didn't break. Thundering down into the valley of destruction, I hit every boulder, every tree, every obstacle. The animals watched but only briefly, quickly glancing in my direction, as I rolled by them, brutally into the abyss. I cracked but I did not shatter; I was beaten but not broken. It wasn't until the last foot of the mountain that I ceased advancing into hell, that I stopped. Only a part of me melted away in that fire. And, as it burned so fiercely, I looked back up and I understood. As easy as it was for me to fall so freely down this mountain, I could also power back up it. As I slowly remembered, how did I get up there to begin with? For the mountain was a part of me and I was a part of it. Now, it was time that I became the mountain and climbed back up.

This is my story. A journey about human endurance, finding inner strength and an evidentiary example that we can pick ourselves up from the darkest reaches of personal existence, the lowest and most painful, and loneliest of valleys, and we can overcome and accomplish amazing things. I went through pain and suffering, depression and severe panic and anxiety attacks; I found myself in a place where I was ready and prepared to end it all, and came inches from doing so. After a year of mental suffering, in late October, as I sat in my dark apartment, all I could think about was ending my life; I wanted the pain in my mind to be gone.

Then, in a snap out of reality, a miracle, I remembered my father telling me as a child, with his hand on my shoulder, "You never give up, son, you never give up." It repeated in my head, and it felt almost as if he were in the room in that moment, looking down at me as a boy. The tears erupted down my face, the loneliness overcame me, I was truly destroyed.

In a flash of nothingness, the sirens rang, the conductor blew his whistle, and instead of ending it all, on the contrary, it was time to start it all. I couldn't end it this way; I knew it would be a long path out of this uninhabitable place, but this place was only of my own mind's creation. I had to take power away from the demons in my head and challenge my mental stability to make my mind sturdy again.

It was if I were fixing the mast and sails on my ship before crossing the mighty ocean. However, I was already lost at sea. So, fixing my sails was out of reach and I had no tools. I needed to learn how to swim, and in my case, I needed to learn how to ride. My bicycle has been my weapon of choice for years now, trusty and true. As I drowned in my sorrows, I spilled my empty cup of empty energy onto my empty self. I was struck with this crazy idea that arose from the ashes of my misery.

I was lost, confused, sad, and lonely. Every day, panic would consume me, depression would darken the brightest of days, and I felt like I was dying, every minute of every day. The candle on the table flickered with its shadow casting on a map of the United States that sat above my tried and unwavering, steel-framed bicycle. AWOL was the manufacturer's name for my bike, which in the miliary means "absent without official leave but without intent to desert." Well, BINGO! I was going to be absent; I was fixing to be long gone, I was going to leave this bleak mindset. I didn't have anyone to officially notify, but I sure was intending to desert, to desert these murky waters and this daunting place for good. And that map, that map was my journey home, my journey to get my mind right, my journey back to life. I decided within minutes that I would ride my bicycle across the entire country, coast to coast, Pacific Ocean to the Atlantic, 3,500 miles. Can you repeat that number: THREE THOUSAND AND FIVE HUNDRED MILES!

On October 29th, 2021, my puppy, Rocky, and I set off on this journey, this long ride to rediscover joy and find mental stability along with clarity and put these demons in my mind to rest.

This is my journey, 3,500 miles pedaling to peace and rising Above the Ashes.

Chapter 1

The Fire Went Out

I spent four years fighting wildfires, on an Engine, Module, and a Hotshot Crew.

Hiked up the steepest mountains from the Salmon Challis to Southern Utah, across Montana and all the way to Yosemite. Even stopped in Nevada a few times just to see how the heat and steep collided when on a desert fire.

We've cut down trees to make bridges across rivers.

Almost got burned over once and choked on too much smoke to breathe.

Walked through the flames, under hazardous trees, through a couple feet of deep ash and smoke so thick you could hardly see ahead.

Got rides on ATVs, UTVs, 150s, 250s, 350s, and 450s.

Rode in Type 3-4-5 and 6 Fire Engines, even a Super Heavy a couple of times.

Flew in helicopters, loaded helicopters, got loads from helicopters, short haul, long haul, ya'll know the game.

Fought fire in the Rubys, Sierras, Rockies, Salmon River Mountain Ranges, and so many national forests, monuments, parks, public and private lands, in people's backyards and front yards.

Take less, take more, close the gap, gear up, load up, clear the line, take five, cup trench, back cut, falling, roooccckkkkk, swinging, moving.

Called helicopters and planes in for drops.

Got a direct hit with a bucket from a helicopter once, nearly broke my ankle and still hiked three miles off the line.

Dug line for twenty-four hours straight.

Got dehydrated, got overhydrated, and got way overheated a few times.

Got minor Rhabdo, hardened callus spread across my palms from swinging a tool all day long, bloody and beaten feet but not a word is said about them.

My tooth fell off on day ten.

Carried 150 pounds of supplies up a hill.

Carried a tool with seven hoses wrapped around it down a hill.

Did prescribed fire behind Bryce Canyon National Park.

Burned piles next to Bridal Veil Falls, in Yosemite National Park.

Slept in the dirt almost every day of summer, except for that one time it rained.

Sat in open fields on our packs during a lightning storm.

Limbed, bucked, and dropped too many trees to count.

Ate MREs for fourteen days straight, breakfast, lunch, and dinner.

Carried an injured crewmember up a mountain for a helicopter flight off the fire line.

Got attacked by bees and covered head to toe with poison oak.

Been in lightning-caused fires, human-caused fires, and even a wildfire caused by a plane crash once.

Drank three gallons of water and at least four Gatorades in one shift.

Fought fire in a hailstorm, snowstorm, heat wave, red flags, and all over the west.

Took the best nap of my life covered in ash.

Almost got hit with a rolling log, a rolling boulder, and a couple of snags in between.

Sharpened a chain, threw a chain, always heard two more chains, and then it was always two more chains after that.

The whole crew coughed all night like a severe bronchitis wing in the hospital.

Bloody nose, runny nose, smoke so thick I couldn't breathe out of my nose.

Singed hair, burnt hands, and tripped too many times on rocky terrain.

Cold trailed, mopped up, swamped, dug, cleared, prepped, burned, and held for months on end.

Saw bears, deer, eagles, rattlesnakes, cougars, moose, and coyotes.

Hot line, going direct, indirect.

Burned a mountain to save a town.

Saved a mountain next to a town.

Got woke up at three a.m. for a flare up.

Worked until three a.m. on an initial attack.

Some of the best laughter on the hardest days of my life.

The most challenging and rewarding job I ever worked.

Witnessed few-hundred-foot flame lengths, a wildfire creating its own weather, admired too many smoky sunsets under sweat-covered sunglasses to remember.

For fifteen dollars an hour and sixteen hours a day, I'll slam line next to the best humans I've ever known, any day of the week.

My brothers, my sisters, that job, being a wildland firefighter is the best job in the fucking world.

***

It was dirty August, 2018, as us wildland firefighters call it: 102 degrees, scorching, dry, high desert. The land was covered with tall and rich sagebrush and dried out cheatgrass, a true tinder box ready to ignite. Humidity was low and the winds were high, perfect conditions for a wildfire to run as fast as it wanted to. During a wildfire, the most dangerous part of the day is mid-afternoon, the hottest part of the day, and when most firefighter fatalities have occurred.

We tried to catch the fire's progression before it slammed off the hill and onto the old, dusty, and partially overgrown two-track road in front of us, but we knew we were too late. The boss told the rest of the crew to hold tight and to stay back; only three of us would attempt this dangerous mission to catch it. The fire crested the mountain, beginning to roll over it and barrel towards us and the road.

In a glorious attempt, my squad boss, Dixon, another crew member, and I took off down the road with drip torches. We were trying to start a backfire to take out the fuel in front of it, using the two-track road as a holding feature. With the twenty-to-thirty-mile-an-hour winds, this fire was coming at us like a fucking freight train in a nightmare.

We started with a crisp hiking pace, in full gear and PPE (Personal Protective Equipment): forty-five pounds on our backs, helmets snug on our heads, and Nomex long sleeves and pants, gloves, and high leather boots covering the rest of us. Putting fire down on the left side of the road, trying to save the land on the right side, and stop the wildfire's progression. Very quickly, that pace turned to a jog. Then, seeing the fire coming closer and closer, our squad boss yelled for us to "RUN!"

Wildfires don't ask for forgiveness. Ruthless, loud, and violent, they show no mercy, taking whatever lies in their path and ravaging the landscape. We ran down the road, attempting to get in front of the fire coming straight towards us. We are burning and running, running, and burning—hot-footing it, following orders but knowing this is fucked up, sketchy, and wildly crazy. The adrenaline is pumping in us at full speed. Watching the fire's swift advancement towards us, we know there is no way we will catch it, but we try anyway. We are Hotshots, highly trained, equipped, motivated, and professional.

Now we have our backfire behind us, beginning to peel over the other side of the road, creating little spot fires on the wrong side of the two tracks, and in the green. The "black" is the fire side; the "green" is the land we are trying to save that hasn't burned. The smoke is getting so thick in every direction and it's incredibly difficult to breathe, which makes it hard to think and to react—dehydration and a headache slam into you instantly as you choke on thick smoke.

The main fire slams into the road in front of us, and our boss yells to run. We follow him, hurdling over a cattle grate, but he stops. "Turn around!" he yells. "Back to the trucks! That way! Fucking run! RUN, GODDAMN IT!"

Now we are running at full speed, literally running for our lives, inches away from being burned over, or suffocated in the thick, black, hot smoke. We just run. It feels like I've forgotten the weight on my back. We can't see any sunlight as the smoke consumes everything around us. We stare downward, trying to stay on the two-track road.

Suddenly, the backfire we set, with bad winds, slams and jumps the road in front of us—now we have flames on both sides of us and the two-track road. One hundred yards later, we are fighting to breathe, our minds on nothing but survival as we choke violently on smoke, running as fast as we can.

Hotter than a billy goat with a blowtorch, we burst through the flames and the black smoke. Through the heat we see the crew and some blue skies, like a prayer being answered. Gosh damn, I think, that was spooky—way too close of a call.

We all hit the dirt. One crewmember is on all fours, choking and throwing up. My squad boss is hunched over too, gagging. I'm gasping for air, coughing brutally. Looking around, I see our faces are plowed with ash, black soot like war paint, our eyes bloodshot and watery, our lungs filled with smoke. But our spirit is not deterred—without a word, we just look at each other, give a nod, and then a thumbs-up.

Bumping out from the flaming front of the fire, we drive back down the road and away from the out-of-control blaze, now too dangerous on this flank to work. We are reassigned to what we dub "Grandma's Cabin." Now our mission is to save a lone cabin, which is tucked into a canyon and surrounded by yellow, dried-up hills on all sides. It is another dangerous task, but this is what hotshots do: we go into the danger. In honor of a teaching that others died for us to learn: Fight fire aggressively, having provided for safety first.

We get into the buggies and drive to Grandma's cabin. We unload and gear up quickly. First thing we do, we get rid of all the trees, shrubs, and flammable material around the cabin; chainsaws are ripping and tools smashing the earth as we dig a trench around the cabin to burn off of. Moving assertively, with purpose, we make the cabin a defensible space.

As we look around, we can see heavy smoke pouring over the hills around us—any minute, we would see the fire, and it would be marching for us at full strength. We set up sprinklers, around the house and on the roof.

When the fire crests the hills around us, and you can see flames, our boss demands we get into the truck and fire it up, leaving the back door open and preparing to drive fast. Our boss and another crew member light a circle of fire around the house, burning as much of a cushion of fuel to save the home for when the main fire will soon smash all around it. After they complete the buffer around the cabin, they come barreling for the truck. Once they leap inside, yelling "drive, go, go, go," we peel off, just moments before the fire closes out our escape route. We blast through the smoke and into a safety zone. As we look out the back windows, we lose sight of the cabin. Tall blazes and thick smoke engulf everything in sight. Another close call, within our realm of dangerous activity, another reason we are called Hotshots.

Days later, as we were putting in line somewhere else on that 200,000-acre wildfire, we overheard the radio: "Snake River, Division Bravo on Tactical 3."

We responded: "Division Bravo, Snake River Tac 3. Go ahead."

"Yeah, Snake River, got some great news—just did a flyover of that cabin. You and your boys saved it. Good work."

***

I've fought wildfires in nearly every western state, and you just never know where the next assignment will take you. Some days you might wake up in Montana and next thing you know, you are reassigned to a more critical wildfire ten hours away in Utah. That was the job—evolving all the time, with constant changes and hard work in extreme and hazardous conditions. A typical day involved digging and sawing on steep, hot terrain for sixteen hours with minimal breaks. We always needed to be prepared for new instructions—suddenly, we might hear, "MOVING!" and next thing you knew, we'd be on a helicopter ride, the crew being shifted to another side of the fire. Or we might be shaken out of our sleeping bags at midnight for a flare-up and just like that we were back on the line. Head on a swivel. Some shifts last twenty-four hours—my longest was thirty hours. This was the job, and we loved it!

The 2020 fire season in California was a treacherous one. There was record-breaking damage to homes, infrastructure, land, and, most importantly, the devastating loss of many lives. This was my fourth season being a wildland firefighter—I had spent my first season on an engine crew in Montana, then the next two seasons with the elite Snake River Hotshots.

The Snake River Hotshots are one of the hardest-hitting, tool-slamming, bad-ass crews in the nation. We were sent to the most dangerous, hottest part of a wildfire and given the most difficult of tasks to do. From dropping extremely hazardous trees, working with aircraft, digging tremendously difficult hand line to risky burn operations in delicate situations, like near homes, it is said "There is nothing a hotshot can't do, even when given nothing to do it with." What made a Hotshot Crew so elite was being able to perform any, I mean any, of assigned tasks, the crew possessing high levels of training. Consistently working in hot and dangerous conditions and continuing to do so at a highly effective, productive rate for sixteen hours a day, on any terrain. After two seasons on Snake River, I decided to change the scenery and learn new skills to advance my career, so I joined a fire module in Yosemite National Park.

At this point, I had worked around 1,000 hours of overtime—in a four-month timespan for two seasons consecutively. This entailed being on the job for two or three weeks of sixteen-hour shifts, followed by two days off (known as "rest and relaxation," or "R&R") before being sent out again. Basically, your summer was fire, and fire was your summer.

The camaraderie within a crew becomes incredibly tight, and the cohesiveness and production rate are a sight to see. You fight alongside one another, through blazes of flames towering above, and smoke so thick that you can hardly breathe, let alone see. The chainsaws—brum brum brummmmm—and the tools smashing into the ground as helicopter propellers spin from above. The helicopters drop buckets of water, planes zip overhead, releasing retardant as you quickly take cover. Accompanied by the roar of fire, the crew operates seamlessly while listening to this cacophony of music, chainsaws, and propellers, that plays constantly throughout. A constant sense of danger keeps our senses heightened and alerted.

Imagine the countless hours of preparation, focus, and work that goes into saving neighborhoods from a wildfire. After the excitement of a successful burn operation, the crew will be tired, drained, and beaten down, but not a soul will complain. We are first responders, and when duty calls, we will always answer that call and be there first to fight that fire head-on. When the masses evacuate, we will stay. When it seems like there is no way to get there, we will find a way. When it looks like the fire will never cease its advancement, we will stop it. It's a job of little pay that yields rich rewards, some of the sweetest of which are the intangibles. Only an unspoken warrior, an invisible fighter, that's been on the line will fully understand how special this job truly is.

***

Depending on the region your duty station is located, the fire season ends somewhere between October and December, and starts up again from March to May. One day, you're up on a beautiful mountain, higher than the clouds, looking over a mighty ridgeline. To the east is pure devastation, a blackened-out landscape for as far as you can see, smoke slowly rising from the ashes of every burned tree, every shrub, and every single blade of grass as a wildfire ripped up the topography. This ridge is where we, with a sturdy saw and handline, stopped the advancement of this wildfire. It is our line—our fire line—a line of fucking grit, determination, and impressive work.

As you look in the opposite direction, to the west of the ridgeline, the forest is rich—a sea of green, an abundance of life and energy. The mountains are pure, untouched, and safe—safe this time, from the devastation a wildfire can bring. Seeing what could've been destroyed; however, we saved that land, knowing that resonates true pride within you.

Sitting up there with your crew—your brothers and sisters—and taking a much-earned rest, the sun breaks the smoke, a bright, orange, and reddish sphere falling from the sky and dripping over the horizon. That sunset, that land you saved, those laughs and high-fives you share up on that mountain, as sweat dribbled out of your helmet and you scarfed down a Vietnam-era MRE cold—well, that's why we do this job.

There is no crowd, no news cameras, no applause. No "good job," or "attaboy." You did what needed to be done, you didn't complain, and you did that task alongside your brothers and sisters, drenched in sweat, your body fatigued, and your face covered with ash. These are the spirits of unbreakable men and women.

We stopped the beast, this time.

Months and months in the smoke, hiking up the steepest of terrains, taking helicopter flights, experiencing near-misses from trees almost crashing onto you, carrying tools and supplies heavier than you've ever thought you could, and humping it all up a mountain with no trail. The belly laughs, the shitty food, the twenty-four-hour shifts, the hundred-plus-degree days. The best friends you make, the sacrifice you lay down, being away from family and friends—from society. Every year, your summer is truly dedicated to wildfire and the firefighters you fight with and alongside of (we jokingly call it summer camp). You sacrifice your life and your time to be out there, in the wild, fighting an unpredictable natural force, to protect the homes, the majestic lands, and the people of the United States.

It truly is the best job I have ever had.

One day, however, it is as if castle doors are slammed upon your face, leaving you outside, cold and alone. It's time to hike off the mountain, and the excitement, the camaraderie, the paycheck, the insurance, the worthiness, and the pride, all of a sudden the season is all over. Every season, like a snap of the fingers, you're laid off and terminated by the federal government. Like a shake of a dog's tail, the season ends, and everyone goes their separate ways.

This moment affects so many wildland firefighters. After six months of going and going, side by side, assignment to assignment, your speed plummets from one hundred down to zero. From enormous purpose and hard work, then thrown into a wild freedom, what do I do now? It's a moment that affects so many wildland firefighters, the purpose-packed days of fire season and then shifting back to civilian life.

Chapter 2

Goodbye, My Dear

In early November of 2020, I turned in all my gear and packed up my truck as I was leaving Yosemite National Park for the season. Shook my bosses' hands and thanked them for the opportunity to work in such a magical place. We had a nice goodbye wildland firefighter party around a campfire. It was the last night our crew would all be together, after spending six months side by side. We fought fire together, day and night, ate every meal together and became a small family, knowing that no one will probably ever see Yosemite National Park like we had. As I started our last campfire with a drip torch, I sat in silence for a few moments, reflecting on our season. Our last night together, and it was the last day I was officially a Wildland Firefighter. It is a bittersweet moment; for a couple of months you can't wait for the season to end, then it ends, and you miss it dearly.

It's goodbye, no more fire assignments, no more burn operations, no more PT as a crew, no more laughs and silly arguments, no more fun on the radios, no more long line digs or dropping snags, no more asking "What are you doing for R&R?" no more training, no more sleeping in the dirt together, no more standing side by side and being a crew. It was time to leave, and we all would go different ways. Almost like a revolving compass, everyone seemed to be going in a different direction. And, just like that, you lose your strong purpose of protecting the lands and people through fighting fires, and you say goodbye to your friends and you're off on your own adventure.

The day I left El Portal, the Western Gateway into Yosemite National Park, was when it all started. On such a beautiful day, I left Yosemite and drove out to Big Sur, California. It is one of my favorite places I have ever touched, as it cut its natural beauty into my soul.

On the drive, I am feeling happy, peaceful, and jamming out to some nice, soft country tunes. I have the windows down, flying my left hand with the wind and rejoicing on the season being done and being free yet again. Only a few hours and I'll be in paradise.

Forty-five minutes from Big Sur, I am struck with my first ever severe panic attack. I can't breathe, my heart is jumping out of my chest, it feels like my heart is beating fast but off and on a regular pace, skipping beats. I feel trapped in my truck, my hands start shaking, and my head feels slightly dizzy and disorientated. I briefly pull over and walk a few laps around my truck, it feels like I can't catch my breath, then I'm sweating all of a sudden and feel even more dizzy. I hold the side of my truck and slide back into the driver's seat. My heart rate is so rapid, it is scaring the hell out of me. I can't see straight. My mind is torn, part of it telling me to keep going and get to the beach. The other side is repeatedly telling me that I am dying.

I tell myself happy and positive thoughts, over and over. I can't snap this feeling; it feels like it is getting worse and worse. Overthinking all of these feelings and the thoughts that I am dying make me panic even more.

I can't calm down. I pull over down the road at a gas station. Sit in my truck for ten minutes trying to breathe. This is terrible. I shuffle in, grab a case of beer, can barely make eye contact with the clerk and don't say a word. I'm trembling, scared and weak.

I get back to my truck, roll the windows back down, crack a beer. After three beers, I finally am able to calm down. Holy shit, what was that? I continue the drive out to the coast and into Big Sur. The panic slowly creeps back into my body. I finally get to Big Sur; I pull over on a beautiful cliff overlooking the Pacific Ocean. I open my door, to do what I always do, run down to the beach, and get ready for a dazzling sunset. Not today, cowboy, my brain alerts me. The panic and those feelings overcome again. Am I really going to die? Why does it feel like I am about to die?

I guzzle down beer after beer trying to erase these feeling. Puzzled by my first severe panic attack, the only weapon I think of is to drink until it is washed away into the ocean. The panic debilitates me, and I stay in my truck for hours, like it is a safe place; I don't even move when the sun is setting. I don't even care to watch the sunset. I just think I am going to die. My heart won't slow down, my thoughts negatively racing, and I feel so strange and like shit. This was not my first panic attack of my life; however, this level of a panic attack was entirely a new experience.

I write my little brother, John Patrick, a heartfelt letter, truly believing this might be my last night alive. I attempt to toss in apologies and inspiring words, as tears rain down my cheeks. I just sit there in pain and cry, so confused with what is happening and why I am not happy and at peace in my favorite place.

After hours of suffering, overwhelming feelings of panic, and sadness, I slam another beer. I finally jump out of my truck and get a big whiff of the salty Pacific Ocean air blowing through the breeze, I hear the waves violently crashing, and I look up at the dark, night sky. I hold my hands wide open, and yell into the abyss of the stars above, "WHAT THE FUCK IS HAPPENING; WHAT IS WRONG WITH ME?"

That was my first severe panic attack of my life and day one for me learning what life would be like with a mental illness. For the next twelve months I would have a severe panic attack every single day, and later be diagnosed with a severe panic disorder. The attacks would come in the morning, afternoon, or night, no matter what I tried to do—I was struck with a panic attack daily.

I can't pinpoint what occurred to me mentally after the 2020 fire season. But my mind cracked and splintered, seemingly beyond repair. It was as if I went from standing on the beautiful, bright side of the mountain, smiling with the sun and proud of how high I was—to being snatched up by the devil himself and thrown onto a rickety old cart, forced to ride down into a blackened mineshaft. The lights just went off, and I bounced down into the darkness, not knowing if I would ever see the light again.

I was drowning in my own fucking head, and it happened so rapidly. Depression kicked in after a few weeks of constant panic. Panic and anxiety attacks consumed my every existence, debilitating and crippling my every move and thought, controlling me effortlessly. I lost all interest in everything I enjoyed doing. I stopped running, hiking, cycling, going to the gym, I even stopped smiling.

The suffering would collapse on me quickly and violently, shredding my positivity and optimism with ease. I would write letters to loved ones, apologize to my little brother for not being the best role model and big brother that he deserved, tears always staining the ink as I said sorry that I wouldn't make it to his wedding. Every day I thought it was my last.

It was devastating to feel like I would never say I love you to someone ever again—I was dying every moment—A piece of me disappearing into thin air every day—can you imagine that feeling constantly running through your thoughts, I'm going to die today?

I was afraid to go to sleep, yet sleep was my only safe haven, away from the monster attacking my brain.

I wanted to hug my mother again, thank her for always being there for me, and tell her, "You're the best, Mom, I love you so much." I wanted to tell my father another harrowing tale and see him look at me and say, "I'm proud of you, son." So badly, I wanted to fix the relationship with my little brother John. Time after time we promised we would try, we'd go for that backpacking trip in the desert, we would talk more, we would move on from the past and be best friends like when we were kids. What happened?

It simply felt like I didn't have any time left, just a dying mind, shattered and destroyed.

There were so many things I wanted to say, so many places I wanted to see, so many people I wanted to help and hug again. But then this volcano erupted and clouded my every thought of happiness and peace ever again.

It felt like a monster took over my brain, and one who was having fun watching me suffer. On a daily basis, and without any warning, swiftly, I would feel as if I was about to faint. I would tremble and shake, have heart palpitations, and feel dizzy, lost, and confused. I felt like I was choking, though a quick small sip of water assured me I wasn't; it was hard to even take that sip of water most of the time. My skin was crawling, like something was fighting to get out of it. My mind would race and fly away from reality like a kite without a string. The right side of my body would tingle and go numb—one second, I was cold and the next I was sweating.

Powerless over my depression and severe panic attacks, I didn't tell a soul how traumatically I was crashing, every day, every moment. I wish I had; for months and months, I quietly battled these demons in my brain. These panic attacks shook me and controlled me for so long, crippling my life. I drank and I drank, drowning myself in dark and quiet rooms, even silently among friends. These panic attacks would for last hours and strike various times a day. They made me unable to function with anyone, and I ceased everything I enjoyed doing.

I remember reminding myself I was a fucking hotshot firefighter—I ran into danger while others evacuated. I was an ultra-runner, running from rim to rim to rim of the Grand Canyon, forty-eight fucking miles, 11,000 feet of elevation gain, all in sixteen hours. One summer, out of 2,150 miles of the Appalachian Trail, I hiked 500 of those with two severe stress fractures in my right foot, a black widow bite and contacting Lyme Disease and still finished the trail. The very next summer, I hiked 2,650 miles to complete the Pacific Crest Trail—1,500 of which were done with three broken bones in my right foot and four to six feet of snow in the final 300 miles; I still finished. I rode my bicycle from Canada to Mexico in twenty-eight days, and I ran a marathon with no training. I've done the 223-mile John Muir Trail four times and rode my bicycle 650 miles, from San Francisco to San Diego, six times.

I always finished, always had a smile and a positive attitude, and I persevered. I was riddled with grit, as the word *quit* wasn't included in my vocabulary, and I carried determination and a stubbornness on my shoulders. I couldn't show weakness, couldn't let other people in and tell them what I was going through. I was too tough to be fragile (though I learned later that being tough is being fragile). I was the rock, the happy, smiling, overly positive and optimistic man, and people counted on me. I told myself that I was too strong to feel this way. Where had my mental fortitude gone?

I dug deeper and deeper, blinded with false strength. After years of being a wilderness therapy instructor for struggling youth and young adults, I had the tools; I had seen this before. However, I couldn't use these tools to my own advantage. I couldn't help myself, so I just suffered. I remember thinking, I'm glad this is me and not someone else. I didn't consume myself in self-pity, just in a bottle of liquor, and I understood many, many humans were going through far worse things than I was. So, I wouldn't complain—instead I suffered silently, drinking until I temporarily suffocated the monster and could fall asleep.

This was the hardest year of my life. I would have done anything to get out of that mental hell, fucking anything. It was brutal, but I was too afraid to ask for help, let alone tell someone how dark it was to be trapped in these feelings. All I wanted to do was to start crawling, gripping onto anything I could that would get me to the cliff's edge, so I could just hurl myself over and fall to my death so I could silence the painful suffering in my head. But there was no end in sight, and that pain only grew and grew, paralyzing me with the feeling that I would feel like this forever.

That's what my life looked like for a year, trapped in a cold, dark, lonely place. It was going to take some tremendous courage and fight to get out of it. In the middle of my panic disorder and depression, I miraculously met a woman. Her name was Jessica, we met while I was visiting some friends in Salt Lake City after the 2020 fire season and at the beginning of my soon to be diagnosed severe panic disorder. It was as close as you can get to love at first sight. After we met, I went back to Virginia for a few months, and through hours of late-night phone calls, we became very close. In March of 2021, I drove out to Utah to see her. I met a woman who gave me a glimmer of the light I had so desperately been missing. But just like a candle in a pitch-black room, her brightness was not enough to illuminate the darkness my mind was trapped in.

***

I finally met her, the woman that purely melts you, just a simple look into your eyes and you can't help but be curious how you got so darn lucky—lucky that she is looking into yours. That quick glance shakes the earth and makes you smile. As swift as an earthquake widens your eyes, she could brighten yours. You simply forget everything around, I reckon you just forget about anything, but her, looking at you.

She steals every thought, unknowingly like a thief in the darkness. Time stands still; if she could look at me forever, I couldn't think of being any happier.

She had never gone backpacking, so I took her to my favorite place, Coyote Gulch. A remarkable spot for her first backpacking trip, and I was surely a lucky man to open a new door of adventure with her. She was wearing my old backpack, burly and big on her; darn, it nearly went to her knees. As we descended into the canyon, she was amazed immediately with the striking beauty of the reddish tall canyon walls. I started a fire with sticks, as she started a fire in my heart; unlike mine, the one she started couldn't be put out the next morning.

What a magical moment, that next morning, waking up, shaking frost off the tent. Her beautiful smile and her eyes dancing as the morning light shimmers hope on the canyon's walls. What a special sight to wake up to, two treasures, one easier to find than the next. As we hiked, I shared stories; she loved hearing of adventures and what seemed to many as long, tall tales. As much as a man can be, I had luckily seen all those tales to be true that I told.

She had never been on a bike tour, so we rented her a bike in Salt Lake City, and drove to Jacob Lake, Arizona, to ride together to the North Rim of the Grand Canyon. The road was closed from the lake to the North Rim to all vehicle traffic, just her and I, riding on an empty road, forty-five miles to the Rim, one of the most majestic natural wonders of the world. She was tough as nails; she had never ridden that far before, so I carried all the gear, and she carried my heart. We looked over the deep crevasse, the endless canyon, the spiraling madness of depth, the upheaving vastness, and we kissed, a kiss I had never felt before, that kiss that just hits differently, the perfect place that makes you wonder how everything could be this flawless and how could she be this fucking great and gorgeous. One of our first "dates" is a darn hundred-mile bike ride, windy, brutal, and cold into the Grandest of Canyons, and she didn't stutter a "yeah, sure," she just said, "let's do it."

Those moments, that moment at the edge of that canyon, I could just sit and bask in forever.

One morning, Jessica mentioned how much she would love to have a puppy. I surprised her a few hours later, with a gorgeous Texas Heeler, whom we named Rocky.

After only a few months together, cuddling in the tent, on one of our many backpacking trips, she put her hand through my hair. She said, "Kevin, I've never felt this way before, I love you so much." She was the rainbow in the storm, the storm just happened to be too strong for that rainbow to prevail. She was like the one wildflower you see on a desolate mountain, up in the alpine zone, nothing else but rocks exist this high but somehow this one flower pushed through and found life, the light after the darkness, the warmth after the cold; she was the most beautiful woman I have ever seen.

***

This is not a story about love. The reason I bring this up is to allow others to understand how detrimentally depression and a mental illness affect everything in your life. The point is when you are silently suffering through depression or a mental illness, you will lose people around you. I encourage you to address these issues sooner rather than later—I wish I had. Jessica and I fell in love when I was falling deeply into depression and suffering immensely with my panic disorder. Not dealing with my mental issues for so long and drinking for so long to cope with them are what led to our sure downfall. It was inevitable, my pain was too deep, and I held it in and drank it away. I didn't want to be around myself; how could someone want to be around me?

I met Jessica at the worst stage of my life, and every day it got bleaker. I wasn't myself. I enthusiastically push you to seek help, to help yourself if you are going through difficult times, because every day suffering is a day lost. Not only is it dangerous to live with mental struggles and not voice them, but it will also destroy relationships with others and most importantly, yourself. We have to start the fight to overcome them sooner rather than later. The largest hurdle is the courage to tell someone what you are going through. I waited far too long to do something, and that painful time, trapped in a negative mind, that time was wasted, and that time ended up bringing me seconds away from ending my life. Through my silence in depression and my severe panic disorder, self-medicating with alcohol, I ruined the best relationship I had ever found. It was doomed from day one, because I was too afraid to tell anyone the hell that my mind was trapped in. I hope you don't suffer silently as I have, and you check in on your friends. You never know the demons and monsters that are potentially attacking someone's mind.

Jess broke up with me because she was sick of how much I was drinking to cope with my mental illness, and I never really told her much about it at all. Even though she came to multiple hospital visits, I never fully let her into how I felt. I felt too weak to be honest about it. The last medicine I was prescribed, Lexapro, I ended up being allergic too. It caused me to be very erratic, unstable, and irritable, sparking severe mood swings, I was easily agitated, and even more depressed. The medicine made everything worse for me and our relationship. I was no fun to be around, I was an asshole. I don't blame her for leaving me, I blame myself for not voicing my feelings and for a doctor working out of their scope and prescribing me mind altering and harmful medicines, over and over again. When I told my doctor my side effects: bloody noses, hives, randomly throwing up and then the mental ones, my panic getting worse, my depression getting deeper, and I was becoming angry, irritable at the littlest of things, severe mood swings and trouble sleeping. Well, the doctor doubled my dosage, and I became the most irrational man. I was so sick of suffering; I blindly followed my doctors' suggestions. After we broke up, I took myself off medication, and after three long months on a wait list to see a licensed therapist, I finally had my first appointment in two weeks.

***

Before that first appointment with a therapist... One night, I got really drunk. I was so fucking sick of living in this mental hell for so long. My mind was tormenting and destroying me every fucking day. This was the worst pain I had ever felt, and I was so darn frustrated—I felt no control. I became depressed beyond belief constantly and the panic attacks all day long, I just couldn't live like this anymore. I grabbed a knife; no, I can't do that. I grabbed my truck keys and thought, I can end this right fucking now. I was going to get in my truck, drive down the freeway, get it up to a hundred miles an hour and without my seatbelt on, slam into a wall and kill myself.

In my dark apartment, I stood up. I was done, and I was ready. A few feet from the door is when I heard my father's voice come down:

- 32 -

"You never give up, son, you never give up." By the grace of God, I didn't do it. I thought about that selfish thought for days. I didn't want to be here anymore.

This was a serious incident in my life and a thought that had never crossed my mind before, let alone linger for days. If I owned a gun, I would one hundred percent not be writing this right now.

It is still difficult for me to talk about all of this, to be vulnerable. I still feel weak, like people will judge me, still almost ashamed about my mental illness. But I do know I truly had no control over what plagued me, and I want people to know what I went through, knowing many people can relate to my experiences.

Every day turned into living in this chaotic tornado. I was sad, but I didn't know why. I was having panic attacks all day, every day, but I didn't know why…How did I get here, WHAT HAPPENED? Why can't I just live and be happy? What happened to me? I'm puzzled and alone, and I won't tell anyone.

I can't feel this way. After years and years of helping others, thinking they were weak for being depressed, or having anxiety, now it's happening to me, but why? Maybe, I had to go through this so in turn, one day I could help others. I won't kill myself because I can't imagine my mother hearing that news. I won't kill myself because I can't imagine my little brother's pain. I won't kill myself because I knew it would shatter my father with guilt that he couldn't help. But no one could help because I didn't tell anyone. I think about it, I can't do it, but it's mind-blowing how much I want to. The thought flew around my mind so carefree, it was disgusting.

But I want to leave these feeling forever. I would do anything to skip this part of my life, like skipping a rock into the ocean in front of me and watching it sink and never be found again. I never, ever thought I could break through and out of all this. In my head I would repeat positive affirmations and words: "It's going to be okay," "Smile," "Think happy thoughts," I went on and on but couldn't drown this flood of lostness.

Depression is like being stuck in the middle of the ocean constantly treading water; naturally you don't want to drown so you tread water, but part of you wants to stop treading and sink to the bottom of the ocean. You walk this thin, narrow, and broken bridge between life and death: I don't want to fall off, but I also do.

***

Jessica asked, "Are you even in shape to do this?" I loved that question; I absolutely adore the thought of someone challenging me. Whether they know it or not, I thought you really fixing to ask a stubborn man if he can do something? Can I do this? I reply, with just a simple, "maybe" accompanied by a big smirk and I say, "Hell yeah, I sure can, and I sure will!"

Jessica and I broke up a month and some change before I really lost control and almost committed suicide. I don't blame her one bit for ending our relationship. My depression, my panic and anxiety, the medicine that I was prescribed, well, it changed who I was, and how I thought. I became erratic, compulsive, irritable, and insensitive. The medicine that was prescribed to help me only destroyed me. I don't think anyone should've been around me through this time. I didn't even want to be around myself. I lost the best woman I have ever had; I lost my best friend. What was very difficult was going through my own mental hell, which I rarely discussed at all with her, and I should've, I wish I did, I should've talked more openly but I didn't.

What was truly the hardest moment was her abandoning me at such a terrible time. I wish she would've been there when I needed her; I mean, that is what love is. However, this was my journey and only I could overcome it. Jessica getting away from me was a great gift she didn't know that I needed. I was already buried deep into hell, it wasn't fixing to get worse, she just helped seal the casket with that last whack of the hammer.

I've heard that hope is the last thing that you lose, but for me it seemed like hope was the first to go.

Dear Jessica,

When we were together, I hid all my pain.

I dug so deep; the hundred shadows of people I knew couldn't truly see me.

I was afraid to speak about how I felt, so I suffered silently.

I felt weak for feeling this way.

I was ashamed of being this way.

I was sad for no reason.

My insides ripped me apart and threw away my joy.

I didn't talk about the million spiders eating away at my brain.

I didn't tell anyone how it truly felt.

I never expressed the deepened panic that struck me all day long.

I just wanted to die.

When I saw you, I just wished I was the person I once was, before this, but I wasn't.

I was broken, lost, and mentally ill.

You will be in my heart forever because you gave me all of you and I was too afraid to give you all of me.

Depression fucking sucks.

Imagine, being in love with someone.

But the only way I could cope with the day was barreling down six beers, to calm down, then disguising it before you came home.

I felt like a missing puzzle piece.

I lost myself. I'm sorry, Jessica. I'm so sorry.

I didn't give you my best because I didn't understand what my best was anymore.

I cried when you said goodbye, but part of those tears understood you.

You were so lovely when I was so lost.

I wish I would've talked about it, but I never did.

I suffered silently, which must have confused you tirelessly.

I'll probably never see you again; I just wish I could've loved you the way you loved me.

CHAPTER 3

Lightning Bust

Remember that life and your character are not built upon how many times you're broken and beaten down—they will be defined by the strength and power that you provide yourself to stand back up and overcome the adversity that will strike us all.

It felt like I had wasted a year of my life, silently suffering, self-medicating and just trapped in a hell I never really told anyone about. I was miserable, ashamed, sad, and hopeless. After a year of suffering, twenty-four hours a day, I knew I had to do something, and it had to happen immediately. And in my case, abruptly. It was late October and the leaves on the trees were making changes as quickly as I. I had almost killed myself a few days ago and I was not going down like that. It was time to get off the fucking couch, put down the fucking bottle, fight back for my life, and rise ABOVE THE ASHES!

I called the Wildland Firefighter Foundation and sprang into action. I couldn't, and I wouldn't continue to forfeit my life, sanity, and who I had become for any longer. This mirror was broken as I looked at who I had become, and who I had become needed to leave so I could become myself again. This imposter of illness in my brain was not welcome, and I was ready to fight for anything to destroy it.

The Wildland Firefighter Foundation's "focus is to help families of firefighters killed in the line of duty," a cause I firmly stand by and support. I left them a voicemail and said, "Howdy, my name is Kevin Conley, I am going to ride my bicycle across the entire country, about thirty-five hundred miles, from California to Florida, and I want to do it as a fundraising effort for the foundation and in honor of our fallen brothers and sisters who die on the line, and I would love your help with setting up a fundraiser. I want to raise money for the Wildland Firefighter Foundation. I believe heavily in your mission and support it; please give me a call back." I knew after making that call, well, now I had to do it. Ya know the strict rules, that imaginary line you cross, well if I said it, out loud, I'm a man of my word, so I reckon it's going to happen. The cat's out of the bag and I must do it now.

Burk Minor now runs the foundation after his mother, Vicki, handed down the torch. She was inspired to start the foundation in 1994, after fourteen firefighters died on the South Canyon fire in Colorado. Burk called me back first thing the next morning. I was sort of nervous. I knew saying I was going to do such a feat, raising money for such a noble cause and finally speaking about my mental illness was a big deal. Burk said he and the foundation were on my team 110 percent and offered me free therapy, which, luckily, I had someone I was starting to work with the upcoming week. Gee golly, that meant the world to me that they supported my efforts. Burk has a way about him, that instantly I felt he was there for me, a caring, compassionate, respected man. They got the fundraiser website up and running and he stated, "We are here for you every step of the way. I believe in you, love what you're doing, and call me anytime, for anything. Good luck, Kevin." I have the utmost respect for what Burk and the Wildland Firefighter Foundation does, and it was a true honor to raise money for them on my bike ride, as I attempted to pedal for peace. It was a true privilege to raise money for my fallen brothers and sisters and for those who may be suffering as I have or worse.

Then without hesitation, I booked a train ticket to San Francisco. With absolutely no training, I would attempt to ride my bicycle from California all the way to Florida. This sounds crazy, doesn't it, well, luckily...I was crazy. I had lost my mind and it was time to find it. I knew I had to get out of this stagnant city and do something challenging. I had to fight to find peace, and to get my mind back on track; to get my mind right, I had to try to stabilize my emotions, my mood, and I needed to calm the fuck down and find happiness again. A simple nine-to-five and therapy once a week weren't going to rescue this disaster that I was in.

I didn't have a bunch of money saved up, and who fucking cares. I'd risk it all to have my life back again. I would do anything to think clearly and peacefully, and to smile fruitfully without this shadow of pain blocking the sun every time it came out. There was no price tag on reclaiming my life. I hope you know that when you crash into the depths of despair, lost, broken, and hopeless, your money means nothing more than fuel for a fire you'll probably not set. Or it could be used for fuel for an adventure you should sail away too. Use your money sparingly but enthusiastically, because you never know how an escapade will save your life, or simply change your path into a better future. I'd rather question that than save it for an unpredictable outcome. Also, this wasn't a gamble, this was more like a "Ya break it, ya buy it." I was broken, and I owned that fact. It was time I fixed myself up. I had two choices, to continue withering away or to evolve.

New beginnings are one of the most beautiful parts of life, and I was eager in attempting to find my new beginning. I was willing to risk it all—to save it all.

I had to do something, something out of the ordinary to battle this panic and depression and these demons constricting my positive mind. I had to fight them back and show them what constriction really was. I would do anything to choke these thoughts out of existence.

It was time to leave. I had to start the long, hard, and grueling climb out of the shadows. I had to fight, I had to put those darn training wheels on again and find that harrowing path home, that home to my salvation, a home to peace once again. There is only one person cut out for the job, nobody is fixing to do it for you, you must do it yourself. I had to fight with every ounce of energy, every drop of blood and water molecule in my body. I had to fight like I had never fought before, like a gladiator, a spartan, a gosh darn Hotshot Firefighter. I had always been a warrior. He might have gone away for a while, but now it was time to bring him back to life. It was time to start sharpening my sword to get back to the battle, the battle for my mental peace.

Knowing myself, I know the power that comes of a long journey, what it can do for you mentally, physically, emotionally, and spiritually. Pushing yourself beyond your means, to extremes, fundamentally you come out a different person. Through challenge births hope; hope fuels future successes. Let's just hope that I'm right.

***

Naturally, I told Jess my plan. I said that I was fixing to ride my bicycle across the entire country, to find clarity, to heal myself, to become a better person and rediscover who I was. Before I left, out of nowhere, Jess wanted to spend some time together. I didn't argue with that, but I was shocked. We spent four magical days having fun again before I left. We hiked up to Lake Blanche; she sat in my lap, and we kissed as I held her so tightly, sinking into such a sweet moment. I thought I would never be looking into her blue eyes again, then we both said, "I love you." I kissed her as many times as I could—knowing it might be the last one, and perhaps the last time she looked at me like this ever again. It was hard to imagine losing these special moments, and possibly forever. She had broken my heart, more than it was already broken, but it seemed we still had some fire left for one another. However, I had to go. We had some nice times those final days before I left, but deep down I knew it was a final goodbye. I told her, "I wanted to say goodbye to you before I leave, maybe we can try again when I get back?"

"Of course, Kevin," she replied.

The day came that Rocky and I would be taking the Amtrak train from Salt Lake City to San Francisco. All our gear was packed, bicycle freshly tuned and dialed, and all my camping equipment loaded up, his Burley Tail Wagon trailer, and of course a ton of dog treats and toys. I knew I was making the right decision, for my mental health. I had to do this; I had to go.

I knew I would get to see Jess one more time before I left, but she never came; she bailed at the last minute, and that really stung. It's truly amazing how someone can affect you like that. She texted, "Kevin, I can't come I'm sorry. I'm going to have to say goodbye over text. It's not goodbye. But I just can't come. I'm really sorry I let you down. I hope you have a safe train ride; I do love and care about you. I'm sorry that didn't reflect when I didn't come to say goodbye."

I looked at Rocky, my sweet little puppy, and I held his head in my hands. I kissed him, as tears came down my cheeks. I said, "I'm sorry, Rocky, it's just you and I. Mommy isn't coming." As important as that goodbye would've been, I understood. I buried myself under that bridge, and it wasn't her responsibility to come down and dig me out. That was a job only I could do.

As I boarded that train, I told myself, I am leaving this shit behind me. I am leaving the sadness, the depression, the anxiety, the pain, the panic, the guilt, the suffering, the frustration, all this clouded and hellish landscape my mind trapped me in—ALL THAT SHIT is staying right FUCKING HERE. ALL THAT MISERY IS STAYING RIGHT FUCKING HERE!

The big thing was, I must let Jessica go completely. Honestly, I should've never got into a relationship when I was so lost, depressed and suffering with a mental illness. The relationship was doomed from the jump, and you can't love someone else when you don't love yourself. I just wish I had met her at another time. We were like peanut butter and jelly; I just brought some rotten bread to the table. The moment I hopped on that train, I was on a mission.

I needed to focus entirely on myself and getting my mind back on track, getting my positivity and happy thoughts revived; I reckon most importantly, my sanity resurrected. I was chained in a mental hell, and I was going to shatter these binds and break free. My life depended on a resurrection that only I could deliver.

It wasn't hard leaving Salt Lake City; it was a little hard leaving Jessica. But then again, I thought how she abandoned me when I needed a friend the most. When my depression and constant panic were at an all-time high, she wouldn't even talk to me. My depression got so deep, I almost killed myself, and no one knew that because I didn't tell anyone. That wasn't a link to Jessica; this was going on long before I met her.

I was going to ride my bicycle, with Rocky, across the entire country, 3,500 miles. From San Francisco, California, to St. Augustine, Florida, from the Pacific Ocean to the Atlantic. Across eight states. This was my journey to reclaim my life, to overcome my mental illness and become one again with this world. The official route is known as the Southern Tier, which was established by the American Cycling Association. Their route starts in San Diego; however, I would be starting in San Francisco, which is an additional 500 miles. I added those 500 miles knowing the coast was a magical place to start and began my healing journey. Also, being a stubborn firefighter, why not make it a little longer, a little harder but a little sweeter.

I would be following the ocean for the first 500 miles, flying south with the birds, soaking in the delicious sunsets over the immense horizon on the Pacific Ocean. This was a great place to start my journey back to life. Aside from my body weight, the trailer, my bicycle, Rocky, all our gear and his supplies, toys, and food, I would be pulling around 170 pounds on that first day.

I had lost everything I worked so hard to become in thirty-four years on this planet. I was destroyed. I didn't have much money, meaning this bike ride would drain my entire life savings; however, I didn't blink an eye. I wasn't concerned with the future at this point; at this time I was focused on getting better, getting better NOW. I had to rewire my brain and learn to smile again.

I wrote a note on the wall of my cheap apartment, in Sharpie, in case I became another cyclist statistic. It read "Always love, always be kind, don't you ever give up and remember to STAY POSITIVE!"

If you reach such a hopeless place as I have, you must break free to understand yourself again. If you find yourself lost, wander immensely and freely. When you're beat down, afraid and hopeless—this is the time you fight with every ounce of energy you can muster, and then some more. You don't stop fighting, you dig deep, and you FIGHT, you fucking roar like a LION. And if you fight and you believe in yourself and you never give up, then you will get there and overcome.

I felt outnumbered by time; this had struck my mind for too long. Out of thin air, an epiphany, a wave of fight came from the deepest pit of my heart. It was time for me to fight back, and I hope you do too. I was utterly sick of being sick, and this was my Hail Mary in the fourth to make a great comeback, my saving grace; this felt like my last shot.

This is my story of fighting depression and mental illness. I want to show you perseverance, strength, and remind you we all have that fucking tiger in us, we all have that fight in us, dig it out and fight. No matter how long it's been, how hard it is, how rough things are going—I promise you—you can overcome anything, ANYTHING! I wish to give you hope in my story and remind you that you can get out of a dark place, and you can calm down and you can find peace; things do get better. No one is coming, it's time to start believing in yourself and the myriad of possibilities, it's time to fight to change our attitude, change your mindset, get off the couch, and become the best YOU! You deserve to be the best you; only you can get yourself there.

As I hop off the train, I start riding down towards the Golden Gate Bridge, where we have a hotel nearby already booked. I've ridden this bicycle six times from San Francisco to San Diego, so I know this route very intimately. It's an amazing feeling standing here once again, the great feeling of an adventure underway. And to make everything oh so much sweeter, this time with my puppy, my best friend, Rocky.

One of my good friends, Leesh Mummey, happens to be in town tonight too. We had met years ago, on our first fire season in Montana. We went out to a nice dinner, but before the food even came, I got hit with a severe panic attack. I told her I had to leave and she understood. I was embarrassed and ashamed, but she was so encouraging. What a gift to have friends that care and are empathetic. I just went back to the hotel and lay in bed trying to fall asleep and calm my mind. I thought what a great way to start this grand adventure, but then again, the adventure starts tomorrow.

***

I wake up, October 29th, eat a quick bagel with cream cheese, and Rocky and I are off. We start heading to the bottom of the Golden Gate Bridge to get a picture for the fundraising site, and the beginning of a fresh start. Those first three miles pulling him on that classic, foggy San Francisco morning, down to the Golden Gate Bridge. I am realizing that this is going to be a lot harder than I had imagined. He is quite the load to tow. We get to the starting point, I play fetch with Rocky, overlooking the Pacific Ocean, Alcatraz, and that bright red bridge. I get hit with the wind, and it feels as though the wind just took a little bit of my pain as it flew by and brought it off to the sea.

I had three goals starting this journey:

1.   To find clarity, fight my demons, overcome my depression, and find calmness to my extreme panic and anxiety. Also, to find peace, strength, forgiveness, confidence, and happiness throughout. Truly, I just want to break free of this suffering and to be the happy, positive, kind, and compassionate man I once was.

2.   Raise a lot of money for the Wildland Firefighter Foundation.

3.   Raise awareness for mental illness and health, spread my message of what I went through, and encourage others to not be afraid, and to speak out and to know they're not alone.

With that in mind, here we go, 3,500 miles. I tuck Rocky into his trailer and give him a kiss, smile, and say, "Good boy, Rocky. Good boy, you pumped? We got this, little dude!"

Let's hope this bike is like my golden compass, and this route leads me to peace. As we officially set off from the bridge, it feels as if I put on war paint heading into battle; I'm instantly determined, motivated, engaged, ready to crush this ride and this illness, and I'm not taking prisoners. This is my life; I'm done with it being out of my control! Fuck you, depression; fuck you, panic attacks; fuck you, anxiety. It's time to slay the dragon and start living again; my time is the only valuable thing I'll ever own, and it's time to fight to make that time special again.

I withhold the warrior spirit; it is time to unleash it.

"Progress is impossible without change, and those who cannot change their minds cannot change anything."

– George Bernard Shaw

Chapter 4

Into the Storm

In the Plains, the Native Americans view the bison as a revered and sacred animal. It is very fascinating how a bison reacts when a storm is approaching. Every other animal in the kingdom, when a storm is approaching, takes cover, or huddles together and some even fly south. The bison, strong and intelligent, looks at the disaster coming its way and marches head on. Directly into the storm's direction. I don't know why they do this, but I like to imagine this is to get the worst part of the storm, that you can't escape, either way, to get that brute first part out of the way. To face these obstacles head-on, strong and sturdy, and power through the face of the storm, to get the worst of it out of the way.

This was what day one was like for me on my bike, minus a couple thousand pounds and the fact that I don't eat grass. I was done running from the storm and the chaos, the crippling effect that all my emotions in my head were violently throwing at me every day. I was done drinking my life away as I suffered, thinking it was the only way to feel better, when really, I was just plainly avoiding my illness, hiding and being weak, running away to that bottle and not facing my reality. That was just the easy route to cope; however, it wasn't helping me at all, it was only making things worse on myself, and deteriorating me at an excelled rate. I was done not living the life I wanted to live. I was done being controlled by this disorder and condition. I was done not having control and being

constantly frustrated in this pit of non-existence. I was done with this
year of hell, and it was time to move on.

Like the bison, I was riding into the face of the storm. To find out
how strong I truly was. Can I overcome these feelings, some of which feel
impossible to describe; do I contain the power, and can I muster the
courage to combat these demons out of my mental existence?

I try to pinpoint what could have happened, which is a difficult
task. I thought about the many deaths among family and friends I have
experienced, maybe too many, or possibly I never fully grieved. Maybe
the mistakes I have made in the past, I never fully forgave myself for. I
held onto not being a good big brother for my little brother, John, in his
youth for way too long. Maybe that guilt caught up with me. Maybe the
same woman breaking my heart, lucky for me she did it twice. Or the few
times I nearly died on a wildfire without ever debriefing on the situation
fully. I have done a lot of homeless work and I'm a very empathic person;
sometimes I think maybe I felt their pain as if it was my own. After
helping thousands of homeless people, maybe my heart still sat on that
lonely street corner with them. Maybe going to a mentally and emotional
abusive boarding and wilderness school still haunted me.

I never went to college; should I have? I don't know, but
sometimes I'm disappointed I didn't, and I don't have a degree. We all go
through our own paths in life and shit happens every day. Or maybe it
was a toxic, abusive relationship I stayed in for far too long trying to help
that woman. I tried but I couldn't, and a few punches in my face, and
things thrown at me down the road I finally called it quits. Maybe I just

ran away from my feelings for way too long. Or, it was a whole lot of things, stirred, fried, forgotten and buried, or maybe I was just simply lost.

Whatever led to this severe panic disorder and this depression, it was time I forgave myself, healed, and fought for mental stability and clarity.

It is important in life to forgive yourself; it's all right and everything will be okay. In moments of suffering and pain, we must become the warrior and not wither on the battlefield of our existence but get up and fight another day.

My father was the one who mentioned maybe I carried the pain of the thousands and thousands of homeless and poor people I helped over the years. There lies a great short story about empathy I'd like to share.

There is a man, deep down in a well. He's sad, broken, crying, desperate, and alone. Another man walks by the well and hears this man's cries from below. He stops by the top and hollers down, "Hey, are you okay?" The man says, "No." He goes on and tells him his problems, and the man up top responds, "I'm so sorry; it'll get better." And walks away.

A little later another man walks by, hears the cries, and asks the man the same question "Are you okay?" The man in the well says, "No, I'm not." The man up top says, "Hold on," finds a rope, and climbs down into the well and sits with the man. They talk for hours; he comforts him and listens to him and chimes in when necessary. This is the difference

- 51 -

between sympathy and empathy; one man just asks but doesn't really care, and the other climbs down into that despair with the man suffering and listens and, most importantly, sits beside him. Sometimes, words are not important; it is the simple comforting act of not being alone that you can provide someone. And maybe a part of me has been stuck in that well with that suffering man for too long? Or maybe I was that suffering man?

***

As the fog swallows the Golden Gate Bridge and the waves smash on the concrete wall in front of us, the seagulls scavenge all around, I kiss Rocky, and I take my first pedals on a 3,500-mile journey. I rip my shirt off almost immediately, smile, and am so ready for this monster of an adventure, and this monster of depression and panic that I will hopefully soon defeat. On the first climb I am quickly humbled by how truly difficult this journey will be. Towing a dog and his trailer is a whole other beast. I'm going two miles an hour uphill, one pedal at a time with no momentum. Without any training, grit is my only weapon that pushes me on that first day. I call my father and jokingly tell him, "I'll tell ya what, Pa, I can promise you one thing—I will never, ever tow Rocky after this trip ever again." We laugh, but I am serious, it's difficult, but I wouldn't trade having my best friend here with me along for the ride for anything.

On the outskirts of San Francisco, along the beach was a concrete wall covered in graffiti. You know how sometimes you're just meant to hear something or see something at the right time? You wouldn't believe what was painted on that wall. It touched me and was so fitting for where I was and what I was enduring. In big, yellow, graffiti letters, it read "When you face difficult times, know that challenges are not sent to destroy you. They're sent to promote, increase, and strengthen you."

I felt so great that first day; I just knew I was right where I needed to be, and I felt inspired. I bought a homeless guy some food outside of McDonald's and got Rocky a vanilla ice cream cone. We ended the day at San Gregorio Beach, a full day of riding to accomplish those first fifty miles. It started to rain as we pulled into the state park at dusk. I rolled the bike and trailer into this not so big, but big enough forest service bathroom. You were not allowed to camp at this park, but I was pooped and didn't care. I've only slept in one of these bathrooms once before, in a hailstorm on a backpacking trip, long ago. Surprisingly, it's not so bad; well, it might be for most, but hey, at least I was going to stay dry. The funny thing is, I brought a hatchet, a just-in-case-of-emergency kind of weapon. And I put it on the top of Rocky's trailer. As I was getting situated, I bumped his trailer in this small space, and it fell off the top of his trailer and fifteen feet down into the pit toilet with a disgustingly loud splash. You just have to laugh at your own carelessness sometimes.

Slept like a baby.

We rode through Santa Cruz. A friend I hadn't seen in ten years, Mike, watched Rocky for the day so I could get into Monterrey Bay a little faster. Only to discover a recent landslide shut down Highway 1 near Big Sur. So, I had to rent a car to get around it. Almost exactly a year ago, in Big Sur, was where this all started. And I was looking forward to going

- 53 -

back there, but maybe this was how it was meant to be. Maybe I wasn't ready to go back to that place quite yet. We got though the landslide, returned the car, rode up and down some big hills and camped on Gaviota Beach, which led to an interesting night.

I pulled in, in the darkness, quickly saying, "You gotta be kidding me!" There was a big sign that read "Campground Closed." I went under the gate anyway and found the only person there, the camp host; she was not very friendly. She told me I couldn't stay there, and the next campground was thirty miles away, down the 101. I told her in a nice way, I'm not riding thirty more miles on the highway at night and requested she call the ranger. I said tell him, "I'm a Hotshot Firefighter riding across the country for firefighters killed in the line of duty." She was not happy to do that, but she did. I set up my tent; she came over a few minutes later and frustratingly told me that the ranger said it was fine. Rocky and I were in the tent, getting ready for bed, when we heard a bizarre noise. At first, I laughed and thought maybe some college kids were having sex in the woods, but I quickly realized that was not what was happening. We were back behind this closed gate; it didn't make sense anyone would come back here.

The moaning noise was the same, every time. I realized it was a bobcat and it was circling the campground, probably very anxious and curious about Rocky, as he was too. Knowing it was not a threat, I enjoyed hearing the bobcats calls for a while and fell asleep whilst Rocky stayed alert; he makes for a great guard dog.

This was where it gets weird. Rocky started growling in the middle of the night. The growling got deeper and deeper and then he started barking, which I've only seen him bark like this once before. That was when we saw some cows whilst night hiking. I sat up and saw a shadow figure approaching our tent with some bags in his hands. He was coming right towards us. I shined my light and sternly said, "Hey, what are you doing?" It just didn't make sense, someone pulling off the highway, walking past a closed gate, then proceeding a half mile or so, at 2:20 in the morning. He responded, "Just throwing away some trash." But he just walked right by the trash dumpster and when I said that aggressively, he paused, then turned around back towards it—sketchy, right? Rocky started barking violently. I yelled out, "WHO ARE YOU?" and this creeped me out. All I could see was this shadow walking away into the darkness, into the forest, and he said, "Oh, it's just me." And then disappeared. It was very strange. I was so pooped from the first four days of riding, pulling a lot of weight, I fell right back asleep and now knowing Rocky's alertness to danger made me very happy, settled, and sure. I thought to myself, sure would've liked to have that hatchet right about now.

We made it down to Santa Barbara the next day. We sprawled out on the beach; I looked one way and Rocky looked the other. It reminded me of Bubba and Forest when they slept back-to-back in that rainstorm. He always watches my back. Rocky chased off hundreds of birds from the beach and chased a blonde woman down the sidewalk. He did this a few times, always a blonde woman; I think he missed Jessica. I did too, but she abandoned me when I needed her the most, and in this first week of this journey she never reached out once, not a call, not a text. I wasn't fixing to call her, just would've been nice to hear from her. However, I was so focused on this journey and healing myself, forgiving myself and growth, I had no time for that shit anyway.

A dear family friend, Alan Haynes, met us at my motel on the beach in Santa Barbara. He was going to help with Rocky for the next five days. Shedding his weight and the trailer was a game changer. I am very blessed for Alan's incredible generosity. It was now time to pound out some big miles and take advantage of this opportunity.

It was humbling what happened when I spoke about my mental illness, my pain, and my mission to overcome it and in doing so raising money for the Wildland Firefighter Foundation. Hotshot Brewery, the Foundation, and Anchorpoint Podcast all spread my journey on social media outlets, letting folks know what it was about and asking if people could help me along the way. It took a lot of courage from my stubborn self to be vulnerable and talk to thousands about my mental issues. I was amazed how widely it was accepted and I was supported.

I quickly understood the power of the firefighting community, as it overwhelmed me with support, kindness, and love. Overnight, in that first week I received at least fifty messages from firefighters, nearly every one I had never met. They were offering their help, laying down kind and supportive words, and reassuring my journey was one for all of us and prayers from so many. I was shocked to see this immediate reaction and support, as it felt the entire fire community was watching me. It was very humbling. I felt like they were there with me, pushing me up those hills, like hauling a Cubie up a mountain, and whispering in your ear, "You got this, Kevin, two more chains." This camaraderie was something unparallel to any, and gosh darn did it feel incredible to know thousands of hard-working, bad-ass Americans had my back. See, I might have started this alone and been alone in this depression and panic for a long time, but when I reached out to the fire community...THEY WERE THERE. In the blink of an eye, they sent me love and support, and I promise I will be there for any of them, anytime they need me as well.

I received a call from Max Alonzo, a man who fought fire in the Tonto National Forest for twelve years. He later moved onto the legislative side working with congressional representatives and senators and the executive branch to get reform for Federal Wildland Firefighters. Most of his friends are still fighting fire, boots on the ground, and his son is even out there digging line nowadays. Max was a guardian angel that reached out to the Wildland Firefighter Foundation for my phone number when he heard of my story. We had a long and great chat. After speaking with Max, it was like a domino effect; he called so many ranger and fire stations, and his connections across the entire country to get me help along the way. He called Barry Johnson, Barry called someone else in the next town for me, they called someone in the next town, they knew someone in New Mexico, then they knew someone in El Paso, it was amazing seeing the connections. The Wildland Firefighter Foundation has a catchphrase, "Compassion spreads like wildfire," and oh boy, did I watch the compassion of my brothers and sisters of fire spread oh so fast and oh so fierce.

Day one: San Francisco to San Gregorio—fifty miles—2,585 feet of elevation gain

Santa Cruz—40 miles —1,869 feet of elevation gain

Monterrey—43 miles —1,728 feet of elevation gain

Gaviota Campground—44 miles —2,434 feet of elevation gain

Santa Barbara—35 miles —1,156 feet of elevation gain

*＊＊

Leaving Santa Barbara, on another classic, foggy, light rainy morning, I felt rejuvenated. I was slapping on the war paint to drop some big miles and take advantage of not having Rocky's extra weight for the next five days. It struck me, weird, this was the first day since I got Rocky with Jessica roughly 5 months ago - that we had not been together. As I missed my little buddy, shedding that hundred-some-odd pounds had me feeling like a bird, you know "light as a feather."

I blasted off down the coast, quick stop for the famous fish tacos on Ventura Pier, down through Point Mugu State Park. I saw hundreds of pelicans in a feeding frenzy and some commercial being shot on the beach. I hardly took any breaks and powered through the Malibu Hills. I reached Santa Monica as the sunsets and the fog and light rains said hello again. The Ferris wheel lit up the touristy, overly loud pier and I kept grinding through the herds of people and chaos of Venice and off to Manhattan Beach.

One hundred and two miles into a 102.1-mile day and my tire caught the wet curb. I slid out going about twenty-five miles per hour and I crashed hard, slammed my head, and ripped my leg open pretty good. My first crash, luckily, I had my brain bucket on, my helmet. I gracefully took a video while I was sprawled out, on the sidewalk, halfway pinned, bleeding on the ground for my friends to laugh about later. My buddies Junior and Cartwheel had put me up in a hotel for the night. We ate Taco Bell, drank Coca-Cola, and laughed throughout the evening. It was very important to me to get a hold on my drinking. I asked them if we could just hang out sober, which is a rarity in our nights together surrounded by palms trees, overlooking the Pacific Ocean. Something about the beach and a beer just goes hand in hand. They understood and respected my request and it was one of our best nights together, sober. I couldn't remember the last time I belly-achingly laughed for ten minutes straight. Cartwheel did his goofy reenactment of a cyclist from coast to coast. Cartwheel is a big fellow, shiny bald head, and a great red beard. Most people that ride coast to coast dip their back tire in the Pacific Ocean and their front when they reach the Atlantic. I didn't do this, but watching his comedy skit, rocking the front of my bike into a wheelie position and then backwards, was hilarious. Chris Farley had his fat guy in a little coat routine and Cartwheel had his big boy on a little bike skit.

It is important to surround yourself with like-minded people, people that are supportive, and positive. A good friend will listen to you and sit with you through anything and drop anything to help you. I hope you surround yourself with people who push you to be better and you push them; accountability and loyalty are a good combo for a great friendship.

The one difficult part about dropping hundred-mile days, also known as century rides or hundo's for slang, was the daylight hours. It was early November, which meant about ten hours a day of sunlight. On average, including breaks, hundred-mile rides typically take about ten hours of time, so sunlight was against me, which forced me to ride a lot of miles into the darkness.

I did another hundred miles the next day, to tee myself up to start making my way east, the next morning. On November 7th, I made it to the official start of the American Cycling Associations route known as the Southern Tier.

The Adventure Cycling Association, who created the route, advertises it as such:

"Experience fascinating landscapes, fabulous food, and diverse cultures...The Southern Tier Bicycle Route is our shortest cross-country route and offers a wide variety of terrain, vegetation, climate, and people all the way across the nation from the Pacific to the Atlantic. The route is rich in human culture and history—ranging from the Spanish and Mexican influences in California, to the ancient indigenous pueblo cultures in Arizona and New Mexico, to the imprint of the Spanish conquistadors in Texas, to the bayous and French influences of Louisiana, to the Old South of Mississippi and Alabama, to a four-hundred-year-old city in Florida."

The Southern Tier crosses eight states and is 3,092 miles long, packing over 100,000 feet of elevation gain.

Leaving sea level on a bright, hot, and shiny day in San Diego, I saw the signs for Sea World, as some people played volleyball and others were homeless and hungry, the cars stacked up in traffic and planes flying overhead. It was a chaotic yet serene scene in such a beautiful landscape. I called my mom to let her know I was heading her way, as "I'm now officially heading east."

The climb out of San Diego is the second hardest ascent of the entire route and I've only been riding for one week. I'm not in top physical shape, quite frankly; I haven't ridden a bike in six months. This is where mind over matter comes into play, this is what separates the weak from the strong, this is where character is built upon, this is my moment to treat this 5,000-foot climb like my depression and destroy it. Too grind through it, and not look back and get to the top like a fucking savage.

You start the climbing on streets, then bike paths, then back roads, then bike paths and eventually thrown out to a beautiful countryside with towering mountains surrounding you and the ocean is not to your lee side anymore. The palm trees are disappearing, and the desert lies ahead. I make one quick stop at a 7-11 before the steep, big climb up towards Pine Valley. As I spread out in the dirt, under a shaded tree and gulping an ice-cold Slurpee, I'm approached by a woman with a young boy in a Superman's cape. They approach me and the women says, "My son would like to know if we can get you a hotdog?" I smile; how kind of this little boy. I reply, "That is so sweet of you, but I'm not homeless." I go on to give her a flyer of my journey and share what I am doing and why. Before they leave the 7-11, she walks back over, hands me five dollars, and says, "We will donate when we get home; what an honorable thing you're doing. We always pray for the firefighters, and we will be praying a little extra tonight."

I felt like an Olympic athlete climbing that hill. The sun was bright and hot; sweat was dripping into my eyes on false summits and never-ending switchbacks. On one big turn, a few thousand feet above sea level, I marveled at the distance I covered today and how high I had reached on this mountain. Riding a bike is much like a metaphor of life; you have highs and lows, and when you reach lows, you must keep pedaling, start climbing again, and get back to the top. I reached the top of that gargantuan climb, with enduring power, force, and a strong attitude. I kissed the ocean goodbye, as I imagined, without pollution, through the haze I could've seen it from way up here. I imagined the pioneers coming West, standing here, for the first time seeing the Pacific Ocean and all the possibilities.

I wrote this in my journal:

"The sweat drips wildly down my face, stinging my eyes, breathing intensively but with purpose in every breath. I rise deep from the valley and soar towards the top. I didn't stop, for two hours I climbed and climbed, snailing my way up, standing, sitting, standing, sitting, crunching upwards, pedal by pedal. I reach the top, oh wait that's not the top, a few more switchbacks and I'm there to the top of the mountain. I look back as the sun starts to drop behind the Cuyamaca Mountains. I can no longer see the ocean, just a sea of mountains. I started the day surrounded by surfers and palm trees, the sweet crashes of the waves onto the beach and the seagulls circling above—only to end it sixty-five miles later in Pine Valley, in the high desert mountains of Southern California. What a fucking day."

I roll into Pine Valley, a rich forested area, in the mountains with a cool breeze and gentle folks. I think about the day, how good it felt, how strong I felt. I think about how it feels like with every climb, every pedal, every mile, every day out here—I am shedding a layer, like a snake, a layer of this pain, suffering, depression, guilt, panic, lost, and a layer of my confused mind; it is a slow process, but the wheels are in motion. Just like the snake shedding a layer and leaving it behind and growing, I am doing the same.

I have a couple beers with my neighbor at the rustic motel; his name is Gavin. Coincidentally, he used to run inmate firefighting crews back in the day. We share some fire stories; he is a solid, kind man, and we have a great talk under the star-blasted sky, as the birds sing along and it smells like fall.

Santa Barbara to Manhattan Beach—102 miles—2,253 feet of elevation gain

Encinitas—101 miles—2,574 feet of elevation gain

Pine Valley—65 miles—6,184 feet of elevation gain

I am still very fresh into my road out of the darkness and my ride across the entire country. Today was my first day officially going east.

Day by day, I will fight to become better. I understand this transformation will not happen overnight. Respecting the fact that I came seconds away from suicide only a few short weeks ago. This is the first time since I was struck with this debilitating condition and depression, this is the first time, coming up that big-ass hill, looking back at what I had accomplished that afternoon, this is the first time I have felt hope in a long time. What a beautiful feeling to connect with again. Hopelessness was a terrible place to settle into as long as I had.

That feeling was tremendous. For a long time, I wasn't too sure if I was going to feel hope again, let alone get my mind stable and my life back on my terms. I was so darn lost, for so darn long. Like a shattered glass bottle, it seemed impossible to put the pieces back together. To just have that feeling one more time, to feel hopeful again, well, that means something, that means I am right where I need to be. That glimmer of hope, that shake of confidence, that proud feeling of "I did something today," I was getting a glimpse of what life once was for me before all of this. For so long I fooled myself into believing I was forever trapped in this hell, and this was life from here on out. I now know that is not true because I saw a little light, and I wasn't fixing to turn it off.

This bike, this road, this dog, these firefighters and this journey were making my heart beat once again.

Chapter 5

Top of the World

Never give up. Never ever give up.

Lightning strikes the Earth 100,000 times a day; ten to twenty percent of those strikes cause a fire. Lightning travels at 270,000 miles per hour; at that speed you could get to the moon in under an hour. Lightning also heats the air it strikes through five times hotter than the surface of the sun. Fun facts!

A wildfire is a natural disaster; however, many wildfires are started by IDIOTS. Don't be an idiot. You can never predict what's going to happen with a wildfire when it starts. Just like with your life, naturally everything that happens in the next three seconds is unknown and unpredictable. In life, you just have to roll with the changes, take a few punches and throw a few back. "Just roll with it." Wind and terrain are two of the main players in which direction a wildfire will spread. There are many factors taken into consideration when fighting a wildfire, and many unknown variables. Will the fire blow up? Will the wind shift? Will the fire jump a containment line? What is our trigger point? What is our escape plan? What if someone gets hurt? Where is our safety zone? Can a helicopter land anywhere close to here? Do we need more resources? The list goes on…Whatever does happen and whatever that fire does do, we do not pack up and go home or call it quits. We shift, we strategize, realign, establish a new agenda, and we keep fighting.

There is no quit in the soul of a Wildland Firefighter, there is no it's too late, it's too early, it's too steep, it's too hot, it's too heavy...there lies no job, no task that we cannot accomplish, and complaints and excuses are whispers from our childhood.

I was thinking about this, how quickly plans change on wildfire assignments, and how I have been trained to adapt and overcome. How could I apply this to my mindset today? I didn't give up and take my life, which would have been such a selfish act in my wallowing self-pity. But now I was regrouping; I stepped back, and planned action. To challenge myself by riding across the country, and fight my fire, my mental illness, head-on. Now, the wheels were in motion, and I needed to see this through. No matter what obstacle lies in front of me, to size it up, to tackle it and with power in doing so.

In life we are bound to have different and difficult things that we encounter in so many aspects of our existence. It is up to us, personally, to not give up, instead to step back, regroup, strategize, make a plan and follow through with it. Never give up.

One in three firefighters will deal with mental illness in their lifetime. Ninety-two percent think it is weakness to speak about. Firefighters are more likely to die from suicide than in the line of duty, yet we rarely talk about.

***

After yesterday's big up and over the Cuyamaca Mountains, the scenery drastically changes as I soar nearly twenty miles down this massive hill, barely pedaling at all. From the rich pine forest of last night, now deep down into the dusty, vast desert. As I pass by ocotillo, Joshua trees, desert shrubs, it is a lightly sprinkled cactus landscape, with hillsides covered with gray-colored, bus-size boulders, and seemingly sparse vegetation on the sandy hills...I'm greeted by an ole friend.

I slam on the brakes, as an all-too-familiar sign catches my eye, like a woman does walking by in a red dress. The sign reads the "Pacific Crest Trail, a National Scenic Trail." Wow, it brings a tear to my eyes and nostalgic feeling to my heart.

Nine years ago, my grandmother, Shirley, passed away. Her everlasting presence is like a redwood forest in my mind, rich, growing, fruitful, and pure. A woman who would make you smile when you were mad and make sure you finished your plate of dinner with a simple look. Her greatest lesson she bestowed upon me was to be kind to people. She died a couple months before I hiked the entirety of the Pacific Crest Trail. And, in her honor, I raised 10,000 dollars for a children's charity in Washington D.C. called For Love of Children. Their mission is to help poor kids learn in school, giving them a better education and get them out of the city and outdoors in West Virginia. Thinking about my grandma as I sit here encourages me to be strong and to smile through everything, just as she would.

What strikes me so purely seeing this sign and this dirty trail is how special that summer was to me. I am reminded of peace, I am reminded of a younger me, a young man on a journey with a belly full of positivity. A young man hiking from Mexico to Canada, 2,650 miles, happy, wild, and free. This young man I was nine years ago didn't understand mental illness or the feeling of losing hope; he simply walked among the trees and laughed with the locals while endearing a positive and kindred spirit swimming in an alpine lake. I wanted to know this young man again; what went wrong? There are so many things I would tell this young soul; however, I would also want to feel his energetic and happy message at this time.

I broke my foot three times on the Pacific Crest Trail, I fell in love with a beautiful redheaded, fierce woman from Montana, I hiked through four and six feet of snow for the final 300 miles. I nestled into the thru-hiking community, one that is rich with joy and kindness and showered in determined, unique minds. I was at home among the granite-lined walls of the Sierras and the enchanted, rich forest of the Cascades. It was one of the best summers of my life.

A few weeks ago, my tank was on empty, and I was running on fumes. Seeing this sign again, touching it, gives me the fuel I need to go on, and tops me off with a sense of peace. It reminds me that I can be happy again and a little more hope is reborn.

A stark reminder. If everything was all okay before, why can't it get that way again? The cloud of depression is dark, looming, and as we see it in the moment, never-ending. However, we have seen the sunshine before this storm and seen many like this pass on by and lead to clearer days. When you're depressed and have mental struggles, you forget that warm sunshine, you forget the spring flowers popping with vibrant colors, and your mind focuses intensely on the dark, looming storm. Seeing the Pacific Crest Trail cast a hook into my understanding, reminds me that this storm will pass, and the sun will shine again.

***

I ride seventy-five miles into El Centro, California. More than a few of those on Interstate 8, with Mack trucks blowing quickly by, but a wide and friendly shoulder, guarded by rumble strips to ride in. The landscape flattens outs, the desert throwing its wide and desolate stance as windmills dance with my God-sent tailwind. I broke 500 miles, 20,000 feet of elevation gain, 3,000 dollars in donations and not one flat tire. The highway has construction as I ride the last fifteen miles in the dark and close to one lane with tight barriers. I can't safely ride on the highway anymore, as I travel fifteen miles an hour; a one-way highway without a shoulder in sixty-five-mile-an-hour traffic is impossible. I quickly jump off the highway and have to carry my bike up a steep, deep, sandy, one-step, two-step kind of hill. Only to reach the top and be greeted by an eight-foot fence. Forced to "try" to gently throw my bike over and then climb over as cars whiz by on the overpass. In the dark, near the border of Mexico, I feel like a criminal on a jail break, but that's what it's like on the road, always changing, always throwing curveballs and this one, these fifteen minutes climbing this hill, carrying my bike, throwing it over the fence and then climbing and jumping down felt like hours of work after seventy-five miles riding.

I receive a few messages today. The first one from the lady at 7-11 before the big climb and she says, "It was great to meet you the other day with my son at 7-11. Good luck and know we are praying for you." The next was heartfelt. "Kevin, I've been following your journey, and connect so much. I'm a hotshot too and have suffered greatly; I sometimes want to kill myself and have never spoken out loud to anyone. I hide it and am embarrassed. You sharing your story has encouraged me to seek help and I just told my family about it. Thank you, you might have saved my life. Thank you."

I'm starting to understand that me speaking honestly and being vulnerable is making an impact on others. I'm raising awareness about mental illness, being honest and open about mine, and these messages are inspiring me to keep talking about it and not be ashamed anymore. I am realizing that talking about what I thought was weakness is really strength. It takes courage to speak about hard truths and emotions. I felt weak for so long, and now I am starting to feel strength through my mental struggles. Truly, I am becoming empowered by my hardship.

Across the desolate, expansive desert, near the Mexican border, a hot and dry 107 miles separated me from my best friend, Rocky. I set off early in the morning knowing I had to cover some serious ground. The desert was raw, the road was quiet, that is until I reached the Glamis Sand Dunes. Altocumulus clouds brought some shade, on the exposed terrain and giant, sandy hills consumed the landscape, a true Saharan desert feeling, but this was the Sonoran Desert. The Glamis Sand Dunes are truly beautiful and unique, the sand looks like tan snow you could sled down. The once-quiet morning now introduced the loud sounds of dune buggies, oversized trucks, RV generators, and the loud yells of drunks ATVers whizzing around the mighty sand dunes. My guidebook recommended to NOT do this section on a weekend, but what was I fixing to do, take two days off? No. In retrospect I would have wished I didn't happen to be here on a Saturday. This is where I adapted a new style of riding. Instead of having my back to the trucks coming from behind and riding with traffic, as you always do on a bicycle, I adopted something I dubbed European style, where I would ride towards traffic, like when you are walking. Nine out of ten of the trucks were leaving the sand dunes, coming from behind me, and I could see for long stretches of road ahead of me. This was allowing me a huge safety pocket and not being concerned about drunk drivers hitting me at eighty miles an hour from behind. After I saw numerous people swerve, all over the rumble strips, I thought I was a fucking genius by doing this and felt much safer riding on this side of the road. When a truck would come towards me, obviously I would switch back with traffic.

At one point the road completely lost all shoulders on both sides. I turn around and an eighteen-wheeler is coming from behind me and then two more coming towards me, and they're hauling ass. I have nowhere to go; I have to swiftly jump off the road as they narrowly miss each other. I had nowhere to go but into the sand. It is mission critical to be alert while cycling on roads; if I didn't get off the road and slide into the sand, something bad was sure to have happened. I nearly died a few times on this section; however, it inspires you to pedal harder and faster to get the hell out of there quicker. Dangerous roads are sort of a blessing in disguise as you're motivated by the threat of getting hit, so you pedal faster and spend less time on that section.

Later that afternoon, far away from the dunes, the road gets quiet, and the scenery explodes. A falcon soars only ten feet above me, and two fighter jets do barrel rolls above my head as I crest a small hill. I had thirty-two miles left to Blythe, where Alan was waiting for me so I could reunite with Rocky. I am stopped in my tracks. I'm surrounded by very rocky, scarlet- and vermilion-colored mountains; many different cactuses set the foreground, under one of the most beautiful sunsets I have yet to witness. I must feel this moment, so I pull over. I rest my bike against a sign, and I walk up a small notch and take a long break. I eat every snack I had, biker hungry, sitting in that dirt watching the best show on Earth. The sun shoots tangerines onto the clouds, then blows my imagination with hues of cotton-candy pinks and purples. Alone on that hilltop, I am in awe of mother nature spoiling me with her red-hot, late-night kiss goodnight.

I drop the last thirty miles under the cover of darkness, truly pitch black but pleasant, as I pedal steadily on the quiet farm roads. Peaceful but disorientating. I don't take any more breaks and haul ass to see Rocky again. I get into Blythe and to the hotel. Alan pops Rocky off the leash, and he goes crazy running across the parking lot. It is so nice to see my best friend again, soft, fluffy, excited, and loving. Alan has a burrito and a bunch of goodies for me, and a HUGE bag of dog treats for Rocky. Alan took care of me and hooked me up like no other; I am so grateful for his extraordinary help the last five days. He drove four hours to deliver Rocky back to me and had to drive back at night, what a guy.

Alan asks, "How far did you make it in the last five days?" I responded "Four hundred fifty-five miles." He says "Well, I don't even like driving four hundred fifty-five miles, so power to you, buddy." We hug and say goodbye; I scarf down that burrito, play fetch with Rocky forever, and fall right asleep.

Pine Valley to El Centro – 75 miles – 2,681 feet of elevation gain

Blythe – 107 miles – 2,578 feet of elevation gain

My spirits are high, and having Rocky back makes them even higher. Well, that is until the heat attempts to destroy me. I get a text from a really good-long distance hiking friend named Karma. His girlfriend, Veggie, and he were living the van life and thumping around the Southwest. He happened to catch my post on social media. He said, "We are camping like fifteen miles away from you." No freaking way, I'm stoked, and we plan on linking up and camping together later today.

It's a big day physically with Rocky in tow so I am back to a slower pace. But a big day on this journey because we cross the mighty Colorado River and tick California off the list and into Arizona. There was a big climb between Karma and me, but knowing they were up the road had me motivated. At two p.m., heat of the day, the sun tries to kill me. I've been struck with heat illness a couple times on wildfire assignments and every time it got worse. Climbing this hill towing 170 pounds, exposed on the hot asphalt, is a killer. For my firefighters reading this, it felt like hauling a Jerry, forty-five pounds of fuel, full gear, and 105 degrees up a mountain in bum fuck Nevada.

I stopped halfway up the hill as panic sent in; I reckon my body was alerting me of overheating. I pulled over, rested in the shade for an hour and a half, focused on my feelings. I felt them, embraced them, and overcame them. This was my first panic attack on the tour; it sucked being stranded under this one shaded tree, on the side of a loud, busy, four-lane highway and feeling like I was dying, again. But I talked to myself, calmed down, cooled down, and got through it.

I make it to Karma and Veggie in the later afternoon; what a gift to see these folks. A long-awaited hug seeing Karma again for the first time in years and very excited to meet his girlfriend, Veggie. We have a couple beers, play with Rocky for hours, and Veggie makes up one of the best Veggie, literally, vegetarian burritos I have ever had. Some true trail magic, or as my mother has donned it, "BIKE MAGIC." What a random coincidence they happened to be in the area. They volunteer to help with Rocky the next couple of days en route to Phoenix; what a fucking miracle. Without Rocky I was able to stomp out a few hundred-mile days when Alan had him; with him and today battling this unforgiving heat, 17.17 miles was a sludge.

I drop some decent miles with their help watching Rocky for a couple days as I ride into Phoenix. Veggie and Karma spoil me with healthy food, big hugs, and incredible support, and family-like friendship. It's amazing how a friendly and warm smile from a friend affects you after a long day riding.

Brandon from Anchorpoint podcast and I are becoming friends and scheduled our first interview for next week. Brandon and Hotshot

Brewery have been a tremendous resource on my journey. My father happened to be in Phoenix, on a golf trip with his friends. We went out for a nice dinner; it was nice to see him briefly before I left town.

I was contacted by Fox 10 Phoenix reporter Stephanie Olmo, and we had a great interview. It was my first time on the news, and I felt so proud to share my personal story and fundraising efforts. It was an honor to talk about mental health and hopefully drum up some donations for the Wildland Firefighter Foundation. It made me so proud as I left Phoenix, knowing my father, my hero, would see his boy on the local news the next night, spreading awareness about mental health and raising money for his brothers in fire.

Here is the Fox 10 story:

PHOENIX - A wildland firefighter embarked on a cross-country bike ride to raise awareness for mental health, and he made a stop in Phoenix.

"Guys, this is quite the story."

Kevin Conley Jr. began his journey on October 29 and people may know the bike route he's on as the "Southern Tier."

He'll be crossing a total of eight states with his last stop being in Florida.

Why's he doing this? He's doing it to better himself and for a greater purpose, he said.

He started in San Francisco, rode all the way to San Diego and then made a stop in Phoenix.

"I'm finding clarity, so much strength, so much confidence," he said.

He's not doing it alone, however. With him on the 3,700-mile journey is his dog, Rocky.

For Conley Jr., this ride is more than just an adventure. He says it's about reclaiming his life.

He's a wildland firefighter who has his own battles.

"I started having severe panic attacks and I was struggling through mental illness, and I was very stubborn and didn't want to speak about it," Conley Jr. explained. "I suffered for the last eleven months going through that."

He didn't like the direction his life was headed and knew it was time to make changes.

"I'm trying to fight through the pain and through doing that, gain strength. So I'm riding my bike not only for myself but for the firefighters, my brothers and sisters that have died on the fire line," Conley Jr. said.

He also has a goal to raise money for the Wildland Firefighter Foundation, a nonprofit organization focusing on helping firefighters injured or killed in the line of duty.

"It goes further than that. These guys have hardships all the time and we recognize those hardships as well. A lot of it is mental health. These guys can go out and fight the fire and they lose their homes when they are out fighting fires and they come back to nothing," Conley Jr. said.

He hopes his journey will spread awareness and wants people to know that they're not alone.

"We are all fighting the same struggle, the same war and I really want people to not be afraid to talk about what they are going through," Conley Jr. said.

He hopes to complete his journey by December 19, his mom's birthday.

Conley Jr. is donating all proceeds he raises to the Wildland Firefighter Foundation.

: Credit for this story goes fully to FOX Television Stations and Stephanie Olmo.

***

Chris, a young firefighter who lives in Tempe, Arizona, sends me a message and offers to help the next day with Rocky. He scoops him up in the morning, we have a nice, short chat and I'm off, across the desert and up into the Tonto National Forest. We meet at a gas station that night; I express my gratitude for his help today with Rocky. I get off the main road, on a dark, back road towards the Box 8 Ranch to camp. It's pitch black, other than my bike lights. A small yellow truck pulls up behind me, slowly following me on this empty, dark back road. I'm going three miles per hour; it's creepy and my hatchet is in that fucking toilet back in California. I can't go any faster; they linger behind me not passing me. Then, finally a car comes going the other way. As soon as they see its headlights, they speed by me. It was three, shady-looking guys in that low-riding, beaten up, yellow truck. I don't think they had the brightest intentions, and I'm glad I didn't find out what they were. It was sort of scary for a few minutes.

The owners of the Box 8 Ranch saw me on the news and let me stay for free. They also own a restaurant in town called Porter's Saloon and Grill. They say, you head on over there in the morning, ask for so and so, and everything is on the house. Good folks, great food. I'm just blown away by their generosity. There is something so special and pure to living wild on a journey like this. It's like the world stops and you just are right there, vividly soaking up the moment and making the most of your time here on Earth. I feel so mindful and aware of every second; it's a beautiful feeling truly living in the moment. The days are full, and my mind is finding clarity.

As I leave Superior with a full belly of food, I am energized and motivated. However, I almost immediately ask myself "Did I make a critical mistake?" The American Cycling Association's official route leaves Phoenix and climbs high into the Tonto National Forest. Most of the trek you're heading in the general direction of east; in this particular case, the route goes nearly due north fifty miles, then sixty miles south, southeast to the town of Globe. However, another road, Route 60, would take you from the Phoenix area through Superior and due east to Globe. Which is significantly shorter and more direct; makes sense, right? I asked a local about my thinking, showed him the map, and told him I was considering taking Route 60, the direct route to Globe, and saving a bunch of miles. He replied with, "Either way you go is going to be tough; hardly any shoulder on both routes and lots of big truck traffic." With that being known by someone familiar with the region, I followed my gut and took Route 60, the straight shot. This was the hardest climb of the Southern Tier and by far the most dangerous. I quickly understood why this was not the official route.

Leaving Porter's Saloon and Grill, I made a quick stop at the post office to mail out some postcards before I hit an unknown, dangerous, and steep climb. Well, the whole route was unknown other than the first 500 miles down the coast, but this section was one where I truly questioned "What am I fucking doing?" and "I don't want to be here." Not that I didn't want to be on this bike riding across the country; I just didn't want to be on this dangerous road—it was scary as hell.

This climb is different than the big one out of San Diego, because this time I have Rocky, his trailer, and everything I need, meaning I am pulling over 150 pounds. The climb starts immediately when I leave the post office. It is hot, real hot, dry, and exposed. As I start pedaling up into the mountains, it is a gorgeous canyon; jagged, steep, rocky peaks, and short desert shrubs sprawl across the landscape as I crawl up through a magnificent carved mountain road. With my shirt off, I am dripping sweat within the first five minutes of pedaling. It's one of those roads you don't understand as much as a driver, but as a cyclist you think, "I didn't know how they made roads this steep." It is a tough and grueling mile to get to the New Queen Creek Tunnel. There is no shoulder on the steep hillside, with a guardrail tight to the road. I am forced to ride in the climbing lane as there are two lanes going up the mountain and one going down. I'm moving two to five miles per hour with semi-trucks and fast traffic whizzing by, and a few not-so-friendly hollers and honks. An eighteen-wheeler is climbing behind me, and the other lane gets swallowed with fast-moving traffic; the truck can't pass me and has to drop into a lower gear until traffic clears and he can pass me. The truck driver nearly plows into the back of me on a blind corner and not being able to switch lanes, he slams on the brakes. I have nowhere to go; he honks, flips me off. After a tense couple of minutes of this big truck riding my ass, he finally is able to pass and yells and yells out his window at me. What am I supposed to fucking do, man? I am very visible, Rocky's trailer is bright yellow, with a six-foot orange flag, and I have neon colors everywhere for safety. These situations are just as aggravating for drivers as they are for cyclists. I do have a right to be here, but I understand your pain.

The tunnel is dark, the road is hot and steep, I just can't move quickly on this grade uphill. I turned on my taillights, took my headlight off my handlebars and added it to the back of my bike to become even more visible, as both flash intermittently. I am so scared going through this dark tunnel, knowing drivers are blasting through, sixty miles an hour, and would not see me from the brightness before the tunnel to the sudden shift into darkness. That quick transition of bright light to the dark is blinding. I get ready to go through the tunnel, then a bunch of traffic starts coming up the road. I pull over and collect my thoughts and pet Rocky to calm myself down. A dark tunnel, with no shoulder, it is quite possibly the scariest part of my life on a bike; to say it is stressful is an understatement.

"All right buddy, here we go." I pedal as hard and as fast as I can. Every second constantly looking over my shoulder for traffic coming from behind, just hoping they see me and quickly slow down or switch lanes. My heart is beating so fast. By some freaking miracle, not one vehicle comes from behind me the entire ten-minute push through the tunnel. It is such a relief, like someone is truly watching over me. When I reach the other side, I pull over in a small turnout and look back; immediately six big semi-trucks are battling up the hill, taking up both lanes, loud and fast. If I was a minute later on this climb and didn't stand up pedaling as hard as I could to get through it, I would almost guarantee I would've been lying dead under one of those semis, no doubt. They would've had nowhere to go, and neither would I. That tunnel sucked, but it's over and I will never have to do it again.

I climb all morning, relentlessly, but at a snail's pace. At two thirty p.m. I see the happiest sign a cyclist can see. A big, bright-yellow, diamond-shaped sign that shows a truck going downhill, saying six percent grade next twelve miles. I couldn't be happier. I soar downhill, relieved after climbing what felt like the entire day. Well, the sign wasn't truthful. I rip down a big hill, hitting forty-plus miles per hour only to round a corner and see this black asphalt shooting right back up another mountain. A false summit of sorts, back to climbing I go, heartbroken and laughing with irony but far from defeated.

It takes me so much mental fortitude on this climb. Thank goodness I had never ridden this road before. There lies a true joy in not knowing when a climb will end or begin. You're forced to just pedal, and your mind can't get in the way of knowing every turn and distracted with how far or close you are to something or the top; you just simply climb and pedal to get there. Mental Fortitude is so important in life; it is defined as "the ability to focus on and execute solutions when in the face of uncertainty or adversity." This was my whole mission, broken into two parts. I needed mental fortitude to combat my panic disorder and depression. It was in the day-by-day challenges that I was getting better and stronger. I also needed this fortitude to pedal up mountains, to pedal from sunup to sundown; the entire route was one of uncertainty and today threw a lot of adversity at me. Towing a lot of weight, in the dry, desert, exposed heat, with no shoulder and dangerous traffic, crawling up a steep pitch for endless miles and thousands of feet. Mental fortitude got me through it.

My mental toughness from being a wildland firefighter, from being a long-distance hiker, runner, and cyclist, it was with me. I was becoming solid again. I never questioned a task as a firefighter. I knew I could accomplish any tasks; it was never a thought of "No, I can't do that." It was the thought of "I will do that" and sometimes "how will I do that," but never "I can't." My mental fortitude from the past was coming back to me in the present, and these hot, long, steep climbs were making me mentally solid again.

When something seems impossible, you need to figure out how to make it possible. I attacked this brutal climb with the tenacity I fought fire with, a never-giving-up and enduring spirit, not ever complaining, and strictly focused at getting after it.

I finally reached the top of the mountains as it greeted me with a warm welcoming sign. "Welcome to the TOP-OF-THE-WORLD," yup, it sure felt like it. It was 3:30 in the afternoon and sunset was at 5:23. The climb packed thousands of feet of elevation gain; it might have only been thirteen miles uphill but it took most of the day. Reaching the top, now leaving me with sixteen miles mostly downhill and flatter terrain to get into Globe, Arizona.

There is a cute, old, rustic antique shop at the Top of the World, and a sweet, stoic old man greets me as I walk through the rusty old door. He gives me some free ice water bottles and I buy a soda and some snacks; we share a pleasant conversation, and he is amazed I rode a bike up that hill as he points back towards it as we talk. He says, "I can't remember the last time I saw someone ride their bike up that hill, but I can tell you, I've never seen anyone pulling a dog up that hill ever." Rocky plays with the old man's dog and we enjoy the rare gift of shade. Rocky and I eat some well-earned ice cream as we bask in our first decent break of the day.

The opposite side of the top of the world is incredible. I rip down the mountain, taking the road and cranking above forty miles an hour. As a cyclist it is fascinating how it just took me five hours to do thirteen miles and now, I tuck and fly down the other side dropping thirteen miles in less than an hour. As the sun starts to hide behind the mountains, I finally roll into the town of Globe. Someone in a big white van slows down next to me. Holy cow, it is Karma and Veggie. I laugh out loud, as Veggie, with a big smile on her face, holds a big, juicy, red apple out the window to hand to me.

What a coincidence, they had no idea, just like the first time we met, that we were so close to each other again. They just happened to be passing through on their way south to Texas. We catch up in a parking lot, and as I stretch, they play with Rocky. As I give them hugs to say goodbye once again, a big, strong man approaches us in the parking lot and says, "Hey, are you that firefighter riding across the country?" I tilt my head in curiosity and laugh. "I sure am." He extends his hand, we shake, and he says, "I'm Tom, Barry Johnson asked if I could help you out tonight." No way, I think, I didn't know exactly what was going to happen. Barry said he had me covered in Globe when we spoke this morning, but I had no cell service all day, so this is a warm surprise.

Tom just happened to be leaving the gym as we were sitting there in the parking lot. Tom is an engineer on one of the engines in town. He offered to throw my bike and trailer in his pickup, but I told him I can't miss a mile. So, I ride, and he drives, and we meet at a nice Mexican restaurant down the street. We have a few beers; a great conversation, and I eat two full entrees. I didn't plan on him paying; that's why I ate like a pig. I go to the bathroom and when I return, he has already picked up a heavy check; it is such a generous thing to do. I am so grateful and if you're reading this... you're the man, Tom. Tom takes Rocky and my trailer in the back of his pickup for the last few miles after dinner, and I follow him on my seemingly weightless bike to the Globe Hotshot and Engine Base down the road. They graciously let Rocky and me spend the night at the base and use the facilities. It is amazing my brothers of fire taking care of me, putting me up at their base and supporting my efforts. I am truly honored and humbled.

Again, I am reminded I am exactly where I need to be. The people helping me along the way, selflessly, authentically, and so generously, these people are breathing life back into my soul. I am amazed to see the bright side of America, the side we don't hear about as often as we should. Americans, hardworking, strong, good fucking people. It is becoming a true honor riding this bike across the country with my causes on display, a true privilege. I set out to ride my bicycle to conquer my demons and raise money for the Wildland Firefighter Foundation. Then, before I knew it, it was greater than me. I was becoming a voice for the community as I was speaking out about mental illness and health. I was inspiring people across the country, and I was honored for the firefighting community to drop everything and support a brother, fighting to get better, with a greater purpose in mind.

I didn't think I would become an advocate for mental health, but I was starting to see that by telling and sharing my story, it was helping others. As hard as it was, at first, to be vulnerable about suicide, depression, panic, and anxiety, I was realizing the impact it was having on others. Them seeing my warrior spirit and fighting it head-on with this cross-country journey and being open about it, being real, speaking truth and not hiding who I was.

I was fucked up, I was broken, I lost hope, I lost every piece of me that I loved, and you know what I did? I risked it all, I dropped everything, said goodbye, and picked myself up by the fucking bootstraps and did something about it and YOU CAN TOO. There lies a great fight within us all; when you think you have nothing left and you keep going, you'll be amazed how much you really have left in the tank. Our bodies and minds are incredibly powerful tools. If you allow yourself to push past your comfort zone, you will realize you are more comfortable out of it than you ever thought.

I leave you with my journal entry from November 12th:

"Thirty miles from Superior to Globe. Up and over, hardest climb of my life. Mental fortitude got me through it. I am feeling very strong, mentally, and physically. Calmness and peace are setting in and I am beginning to feel some true clarity.

Love is the most important thing in life. It can move mountains and shake your soul. It can light fire from under you and inspire great movements. If you believe in one thing, let it be love. Where does love start? It starts from within; you must love yourself in order to love others. I hadn't loved myself in a long time and I was starting to feel it again. It was through pushing myself every day, waking up and pedaling, getting after it, pedaling my ass off no matter the weather, terrain, or how I felt, I endured. Building my confidence up brick by brick, I was putting my house of self-love back together and I was starting from scratch, the trick was...I was starting. When the Big Bad Wolf came and blew my house of existence down, I was left with two choices. To give up, as I almost did, or to rebuild. As I began to rebuild, day by day I was losing my fear of the Big Bad Wolf of depression and panic coming back and blowing my house down ever again. He may have lingered in the nearby forest and popped his head out to say hello; however, I was slowly not paying attention to him and focusing my energy on rebuilding my house. I was building stronger walls of positivity, a stronger foundation of love and through time I was building a sturdy fence of purpose and passion. And soon, I will throw up a steel roof of confidence, peace, and truth. Build up your house and protect that fucking thing.

I am putting a ton of energy and love out to the world; I am humbled watching it flow so effortlessly back into my soul."

"Your mind is like a parachute; it only works if it's open."

-Frank Zappa

Chapter 6

White Blazes

You might ask yourself, out of all the ways to deal with depression and mental illness, why did I choose riding my bicycle 3,500 miles across the country. The simple response is I believe it was a subconscious decision. I knew I had to leave Salt Lake City, as I felt so close to my heart, I had to challenge myself to get out of this dark place. I didn't realize this until recently, but the greatest gift I was receiving on this bike was solitude. When I am out in the middle of nowhere and sixty miles from a town, with no cell service, no friends, and no escape. When my issues confront me, and I am smashed with the rise of panic or my depression is intensifying and knocking on my door, I have no escape and I am forced to sit with these feelings, these emotions, and to cope with them, to understand them and work through them. This is helping me so much; being out here on the day-to-day grind is making me stronger. My only escape is to keep pedaling and feel the feels. I am destroying my worst enemy and becoming my own best friend again.

I wasn't on medication, and I was not escaping with alcohol anymore. I was building back my tool shed; I was understanding myself better. Self-awareness is fucking critical. I was becoming aware of triggers, things that would set on panic and depression, and I was identifying with it and not allowing myself to be afraid of it anymore. I was done running. I was respecting my feelings, growing awareness about my inner self, like asking myself what is my brain doing? Why is this happening? I started to understand my mental illness better and work with it, and not against it. I was growing a pattern of mindfulness and making it a point to do two things on a daily basis that seem to tremendously help calm me down.

One: I would tell myself a few times a day, and sometimes over and over in my head, what I was grateful for. These positive and happy thoughts seemed to cast shade on the negative ones, and it's such a healthy reminder that we should all practice. I would repeat, "I am grateful for the privilege to be able to see the world, not only with my eyes but with my bike," and then think, "Wow, how cool is that? Who created bikes? That's fucking rad! It's so beautiful out here. I am grateful for my family, my friends, my PUPPY, ROCKY!" And so on, and these positive thoughts would drown the others that I struggled with for so long.

Do you have a roof over your head?

Do you have food?

Running water?

Someone to call?

Do you have a jacket to throw on when you're cold?

There are always things to be grateful for; think about them, recite them to yourself, fuck, go yell your gratitude off a mountainside. Those are some simple ones, water, shelter, clothes, but when I would actually spend time with what am I really grateful for, I would ponder happy things for a while and it was beautiful. Gratefulness is a true key to happiness.

Two: Mindfulness

Now this is a topic people write books about, and that is not my intention here. I was becoming more mindful. An area I focused on fruitfully, that I believe is very meaningful, was how I interacted with others, how I treated people and the message I spread to the world. I want to be fully engulfed in the moment, being kind to the people I encountered on my bike ride. Typically, if you're kind to people, they will be kind to you; this hit me in the face tenfold, and made me grateful, again. I tried to be more mindful of my message on news channels, social media, and podcasts. I had a story I wanted to share, and I wanted to share it correctly and authentically. It was important to me to be vulnerable and speak truth about my mental illness and hopefully open the doors for others to do so, especially my firefighting brothers and sisters and anyone else that was listening. And raising money for the Wildland Firefighter Foundation; as I hung flyers across the country in gas station windows, rest stops, restaurants, and handed hundreds out to people, I was very mindful of how I presented myself. I have the utmost respect for the foundation; it was important I was mindful with my attitude, behavior, and message when raising money in honor of them and my fallen heroes. Staying present was nearly effortless on my journey, which can be difficult to achieve. And, being conscious of my feelings and thoughts, mindful of what I was going through and accepting them, good or bad, happy or sad, I stayed mindful and didn't put up walls of denial. I broke walls down and saw the world from a new, calming perspective.

Take what you will from that; it is something to think about. What are you grateful for? Are you mindful, are you enhancing your mindfulness abilities, do you understand the states of self-awareness and mindfulness? It's some good stuff, and it helped me enormously.

Breathe in the moment. Soak it in. Be authentic. Be compassionate. Love others and you will find peace.

***

TEN YEARS AGO, my mother drove me down a rocky, dirt road into the mountains of Northern Georgia and onto Springer Mountain. She gave me a big hug, kiss, and wished me luck as I took my first steps on the famous Appalachian Trail, a dirt footpath stretching along fourteen states, from Georgia to Maine, starting here at Springer Mountain and ending at the "Greatest Mountain," Katahdin.

A couple years before I stepped foot on this long walk, I stepped into a nursing home with my mother to see my grandfather, Poppy. Poppy had a brain leakage, dementia, and he was dying. Only two hours from my parents' home and I never really made it up there and visited. I was a selfish young twenty-one-year-old, and a punk for certain. My mother urged me to go see him all the time, and this time it was too late. Why did I wait so long? He was on his last days here on Earth. He was the only grandfather I ever had and the best grandfather a boy could've asked for. And where was I when he needed me? I didn't visit; I was out partying and wasting my days away while he was suffering. He could barely move; he couldn't take care of himself and didn't speak. On that last visit, he only said one thing. As I handed him small pieces of chocolate, he just snatched the whole bar. We tried to play chess, but he just stared at you with these big, beautiful blue eyes. It is so hard to write this. I knew I had fucked up; why hadn't I come sooner. What was wrong with me?

My mother gave him a big hug and kiss; then I came in to give him the same. I looked at him and said, "Poppy, I love you." And his response has haunted me. I see his face like it was yesterday, him hunched over, in a bib, wrinkled, withering, and dying in a hopeless environment and he said, "I thought you did."

That was the last thing the best man I never fully knew said to me. He died a week later. My Poppy was a World War II and Korean War veteran and pilot. He could make you laugh when you were sad and made you feel special for no reason. He was the epitome of the Greatest Generation.

When he died and we went up to the funeral and burial, I was struck with such guilt and sadness, and true frustration in my selfish behavior. He was honored by the military, rightfully so, the twenty-one-gun salute, the American flag ceremony, a great sign of respect. One of the last soldiers in his platoon who was still alive drove seven hours to pay his respects after not seeing Poppy since the war; that's some honor and respect I have never seen. As the casket was lowered, it landed such a punch in my gut.

I couldn't get this image out of my head, him in that wheelchair, my incredible Poppy, so weak, frail, and he only said this one thing to me: "I thought you did."

When we got home from the funeral, I grabbed every old VHS home movie I could. I grabbed a bottle a liquor, a glass of ice, and turned off the lights in the basement as I put one of the old home movies in the VCR.

I wanted to bring my grandfather back to life, to see the younger, smiling, joyful Poppy I knew as a boy. I didn't want to remember the way I last saw him, and I didn't know how to deal with this. I was reminded of so many happy memories with him through these home videos. He would play wiffle ball with me for hours, take me fishing down at the pier, and always get me the biggest ice cream cone afterwards covered with jimmies or chocolate sprinkles. When I was a boy, we went to a pharmacy for something. I stole a piece of candy, not knowing what I was doing. When we got outside, I opened it and ate it. Poppy looked at me and said, "Where did you get that?" I said, "The store." He told me that is stealing, and it is wrong. He handed me a dime and told me I must go back into the store and apologize and pay them. I'll never forget it because he made me go in alone. I was so scared. It was a lesson of honesty that I have valued ever since.

I also remember hiding under a bed for hours because he told me, "I'm going to beat you until you're black and blue." We laugh about that nowadays; he never hit me once. He was a kind, nurturing, hardworking, highly respected, and quick-witted grandfather. Losing him, was when I finally understood the saying, "You don't know what you got, until it's gone."

I would torture myself with these home movies and reliving the last time I saw him. I would torture myself for being so selfish and not visiting him sooner and more frequently. It tore me up. I ran away from my problems, selfishly so. I drank and drank, and fucking drank; it was disgusting. I was depressed, sad, and didn't have tools to cope and didn't want to talk about it to anyone.

My relationship with my parents became torn, battered, and broken, and was filled with hateful words. I lost every connection with my father. And both my parents seemed to lose hope in me as I got in trouble a few times and drank my early twenties away, with lights off, in a dark basement with a bottle of vodka.

Things happen for a reason. And, when they do, I hope you jump on the opportunity.

It had been a couple years since my grandfather died and I drowned myself in alcohol through my depression. Then, my dad's mother, Shirly, my grandmother, was moving into a nursing home a couple miles away from my parents' home.

This was my opportunity for a sort of redemption. I was not there for my grandfather, so it was my chance to be there for my grandmother. And I was. I went down to Heritage Hall nursing home to visit her EVERY SINGLE DAY.

When I was out of touch with reality, and trapped in self-pity and not grieving properly, and drowning in liquor bottles and bad decisions...She breathed life into my soul and fire into my spirit; as her life was coming to an end, she was giving me a new beginning on my life. Walking into a nursing home is typically a sad environment, but going to see my grandma was not. When I would walk into her room, she would always be in her bed and sometimes a wheelchair; normally the bed and she would light up like the Fourth of July. The way she would just say "oh boy." And sit up, smile from ear to ear, and be so excited to see me and give me the sweetest, tightest squeeze and always whisper something like "I love you," or "I'm so glad you're here," into my ear.

While visiting my grandma all the time, my father would come very frequently too. And, through this rough time on him, we bonded, our relation grew back together, and we shared something special. Those days with Grandma were some of the fondest memories of my life.

I tell you this story because it was another point in my life when I went through mental problems. Depression is dark and unforgiving. And it was time for me to let go. I decided to trade in those old VHS movies for hiking boots and a backpack, and trade in those liquor bottles for a Nalgene and a sleeping bag, and instead of hibernating in that dark basement wasting my life away to grab a tent, a headlight, and venture off into the great outdoors. To look at the stars and not the ceiling and let go of my pain and feel the sunshine.

On a cold, rainy night in February of 2012, I came home late from the bars. I ran up to my parents' bedroom, bursting into tears and said, "I can't live like this anymore."

And that is why I hiked the Appalachian Trail. The people, the challenge, the views, the sunsets, and the self-growth that happened in those 2,150 miles backpacking saved and changed my life.

Now, October of 2021, nearly 10 years later... I'm inches, moments away from killing myself. I hear my father's voice echoing in my head, "You never give up, son; you never give up." A lightbulb goes off and I decide to ride across the country. I imagine my subconscious recognized what happened all those years ago and catapulted me onto this new trajectory.

The ending of the Appalachian Trail was sweet as the forest was coated with autumn flavors, a cool breeze, dear friends, and the bittersweet feelings of accomplishments and goodbyes up in Maine. My grandmother passed away a few months after I reached Mount Katahdin and finished that long walk in the woods.

I was refreshed, a new man, a different spirit, confident, and a positive and strong attitude was enthralled into me. And when she passed away, I didn't drink, I didn't run, I didn't watch old home movies and beat myself up. I grieved, reasonable, I lost my best friend, but I processed it in a healthy way. I was so proud to get to know her so well. She taught me so many lessons in that nursing home, and it brought my father and me back together, as a father and son, and we became friends.

I urge you to take your moments with people intentionally, and meaningfully; you never know when it will be the last time. Forgive people. Forgive yourself.

You only have one family; it is important you make the most of the time you're granted with them. Never be afraid to tell people you love them. Don't hold grudges; give people a second chance.

Never question that eight-hour drive to go see your grandpa. Live spontaneous and with love. You cannot change what has happened; yesterday is yesterday. Today is today, and how today unfolds is up to you. Breathe in the fresh air and live in the moment.

Over 750 miles into this bike ride and I know I have two very special guardian angels watching over me and keeping me safe.

Just like the Appalachian Trail, that big challenge so long ago saved my life...I'm seeing this giant challenge starting to do the same.

Forgive yourself and let go.

"To forgive is to set a prisoner free and to discover that prisoner was you." -Lewis B. Smedes

Chapter 7

Sacred Lands

With mountains piercing off in the distance, the land before me was dribbled with soft hills, cracked concrete, and a gentle breeze. The sun was bright orange, the only thing in the sky and beating directly down on me, giving me warmth on this sacred land as I passed by the Yucca, mesquite, desert ironwood, and the oddly standing saguaro cactus, which are beautiful as they shoot up towards the heavens. The next fifty miles I would be riding across the San Carlos Apache Reservation.

Apache is the word the Spanish called the natives, which meant "enemy." The Apache called themselves Inde, N'de, which means "the people."

His given name was Goyahkla, "The One Who Yawns," but later, after proving himself a fearless warrior in Apache raids against Mexicans, he earned the title and name of Geronimo. When he was a young man, his mother, wife, and his three young children were murdered by Mexicans. He said, "I had lost all." Geronimo was best known for his skills as a shaman, a medicine man, and it was believed he had supernatural powers. They said that he could heal the sick, create rainstorms, see the future, slow time, and avoid bullets. When his family was murdered, he went to the mountains to mourn, where a spirit came down and told him, "I will take the bullets from the guns of your enemies—and no bullet will ever kill you." He spent most of his life at war, to protect the Apache lands, freedoms, and culture. He was shot fifty times and at point blank range and not one of those bullets killed him. Was that spirit he heard as he was grieving in the mountains real? Sure came to be true.

After thirty years of fighting for his people, on September 4th, 1886, the legendary warrior Geronimo surrendered in Skelton Canyon. He was the last Indian leader to surrender to the United States. He is thought to have been the toughest of Apache ever, and then we hunted him down and dragged him off his people's land, locked him up, and used him as a guinea pig for tourism in Florida; what a fucking disgrace and shame. He was held as a prisoner of war for the next twenty-three years in Florida, Alabama, and Oklahoma. He died of pneumonia. He never got to see these amazing sacred lands ever again, the very land I am riding across today. It's hard to imagine how we treated the Apache, killing them, slaughtering them, then forcing them to move wherever we said, burning down villages and destroying their history. I have so much respect for the Apache as I look up at the sky and say thank you, thank you for having me on your sacred lands.

On his deathbed, his last words were, "I should never have surrendered. I should have fought until I was the last man alive." I thought about those words, how powerful, and what a regret it must have been before he died. I related it to my story, how I almost surrendered and gave up on life because I was just done silently suffering. I didn't surrender; I got as close as I could get to it, but I didn't, and I took on the warrior spirit and decided to fight back.

I can't understand what we have done to these resilient, brave, intelligent, beautiful people over the last few hundred years; it's truly sad.

I was warned by a couple white folks in Globe about potential danger on the reservation, suggested to ride through it, not camp there, and ride cautiously. I took that with a grain of salt. When I crossed onto the reservation, the wind started to howl, pushing me from behind. It was almost as if I could hear the whispers of the natives who lived here for thousands of years. I felt something special on these sacred lands, as I looked across the rough desert, I imagined Apache with bows and arrows, hunting buffalo and antelope, and the women gathering wild plants, farming. It was said, "An Apache women could find water where others would die of thirst."

Twenty miles into the holy lands is a sign that says "Dripping Spring Holy Ground." Rocky and I take a nice, shaded break here. I rest, let sand run through my fingertips, and daydream about the special place I am at. I let Rocky loose out of his trailer, to play fetch and roam. He loves the desert, something about the sand, he just sprints in big, wide-open circles, almost looking like he's smiling. He's a happy dog, and maybe the most adventurous Texas Heeler ever. After a nice break we drop off the high mesa and down into Peridot, where we stop at the Apache Burger Travel Center.

It's one p.m., it's hot, and I am hungry. As I am getting Rocky out of the trailer and throwing on his leash to go inside, a nice, young Apache man approaches me. He has this very welcoming and grand smile. As he looks at my bicycle, trailer, and all my gear, he says, "Hey, man, can I ask what you're doing?" I smile and say, "Yes, I'm riding my bike across the country with my dog. This is Rocky; I'm a firefighter and raising money for charity." "Wow, that is so cool; can I shake your hand?" he asks. "Of course." He tells me his name is Renaldo and runs to his car to get his wife and a camera to take a picture together. He hands me twenty dollars, wishes me safe travels, and says the Apache are rooting for you and praying for you. I give him the fundraiser flyer and he says he will donate when he gets paid soon. A nice hug and handshake and it's now lunchtime.

That was my first impression of who the Apache were. I already respected Native Americans, and that warm welcome, the smile, the hug, the money for lunch, and the prayers Renaldo gave me, raised my respect even more. What a warm welcome to their Sacred Lands.

It turns out, Renaldo is a Councilman of the White Mountain Apache Reservation. He sends me nice, kind text messages for the rest of my journey. That was my first encounter with an Apache, and it was so special. He was so fascinated by me and my journey and I was so fascinated by him, and his journey.

The Apache Burger is packed, and I'm tucked in the back of a fifteen-person line. There is a wide, burly man, linebacker size, in front of me. Remember, I did that interview with FOX 10 in Phoenix, and it happened to be on the news last night. He turns around, sees my dog, and then he looks up at me.

With a gentle smile, he asks, "Hey, are you that firefighter riding across the country for charity; is that Rocky?" I laugh, smile back, and reply, "Yes, sir," kind of shocked, not having that happen to me before. He turns around facing the fifty-odd people in the restaurant and yells, "Hey, everyone, this is the firefighter riding across the country for firefighters that died, with his dog, Rocky!" A shy moment but humbling as everyone starts clapping.

He is a tribal youth leader with a group of eight or nine teenagers; they had just left a gathering, a parade event, and were heading home.

After I order food, I head outside to wait with Rocky. Shortly after, he approaches me as I'm sitting in a splinter of shade with Rocky and expresses, "Kevin, we would like to do something for you." The kids shuffle off the bus, one by one, and one carrying a drum. We are in the middle of nowhere at a glorified truck stop, with people constantly coming in and out, a chaotic scene of sorts. He goes on, "We want to sing you a song, it's called 'Going Home,' an ancient Apache song for warriors and hunters, wishing them safe travels to get back home."

I'm humbled, honored, and taken aback by this gesture...As one boy beats on the drum, they all sing in their native tongue; it is beautiful. I had no understanding of the words, but I can feel the energy, the power, and I'm overcome with emotion. I wipe tears from my cheeks and put my sunglasses on. Something just moves me as they chant; the song holds so much more, like the words are coming alive as they sing them. About ten to twelve minutes later, they finish.

I shake all the kids' hands and tell them thank you. I hug the tribal leader and he tells me, "That will keep you safe, brother, we will all pray for you, the entire Apache Nation will pray for you and we are honored to meet you. I love what you're doing, keep pedaling."

Keep pedaling I will. It doesn't get more special than that. That was one of the coolest things to have ever happened to me, perfect place, and the perfect time, the stars aligned, and assured me yet again I was right where I needed to be.

I would've never guessed in a hundred years I would have Apache Indians singing me an ancient song, in their language, on their sacred lands, for my safe journey. It was powerful and meant the world to me. The Apache people have warm, rich smiles, hardened skin and souls, and welcomed me with so much love, I truly felt at home with how they treated me.

I waited two hours for those cheeseburgers, and after the drum circle a dozen or so people came over and shook my hand, pet Rocky, and bombarded me with twenty-one questions.

In awe of what happened today, I pedal into the sunset with a grand smile of gratitude. I'll never forget looking all around as I pedal graciously through the Apache lands, just dazzled as goosebumps come up my spine in shock of the moment I just had. Overwhelming joy, as I yell to the clouds, "WOW!"

I hop a fence, hide my bike, and camp on a hillside overlooking the sacred lands. I recall the moment of them chanting as the sun kisses the horizon and spits red, pink, and orange rockets in every direction. I am so humbled and enlightened on how special today was and this sunset packs a punch that gives me goosebumps again, and tears of joy. Rocky and I climb up a small hill and perch on a rock outcropping, astonished by the sunset as we gaze over the vast desert and the rising of the Gila and Pinaleno Mountains.

We hiked off the amazing sunset spot, back to camp; as I cooked and stirred my dinner, I endlessly threw the ball for Rocky. The moon lit up the desert floor and the stars seemed like you could grab them as they danced across the big, open sky. I went to bed at 7:45, under a blanket of shiny stars, a heart filled with love and a spirit high as the mountains...

What a special day to be on the Southern Tier.

The next morning has quite the interesting start. A few miles outside of Bylas, Arizona I get a flat tire on Rocky's trailer. I grab my pump, thinking it'll be a quick fix, then I realize that my pump doesn't work for his tire and somehow, I didn't even think to pack an adapter or even know I needed one. Big mistake, but you live, and you learn. I can't ride with his trailer having a fully flat tire, so I stick my thumb out, trying to get a ride to a gas station a few miles down the road.

And, wham, the first car pulls over and offers help. It's a small, banged-up, Ford Explorer. The back window is shattered and gone, glass all over the back seat, and the seats are torn to shreds. I will not mention this man's name. The first thing he asks me is if I have any knives or guns. I say no. He also says his car can't go into the park position, so he has to park it at the perfect angle and put a rock behind the tire. It is sketchy but I need help, oh wait it gets sketchier. When I load my bike, trailer, and get Rocky in and finally sit down, he looks at me, with his head sideways, beady, bloodshot eyes and says, "Oh yeah, by the way, I'm intoxicated." It's eight o'clock in the morning. I offer to drive but he says he does this every day. He tells me sad tales on that fifteen-minute drive to town, about all his friends are dead, in prison, or in rehab, and he doesn't have any friends left around. He says his girlfriend is a drunk, he is a drunk, and his parents don't like him around anymore.

I didn't judge him; I can't imagine living in the world he does. He was a nice man to me, helpful, kind, funny, it was just sad to see how alcohol ruined his life, with himself and his family. How could I judge him, when I used alcohol to cope through my issues and it ruined part of mine, especially with Jessica.

I came to realize that alcohol was a pretty big issue on the reservation, and I saw it firsthand when we arrived at a place called Red's Convenience Store. I got him some gas and was able to pump up my tire. He gave me a hug, wished me safe travels, and said, "See you when I see you." I liked that saying.

As Rocky and I huddle in the shade eating breakfast, another Apache at the gas station hears of our tale. It seems the entire Apache tribe knows about Rocky and me. He pulls over, shakes my hand, and gives me five dollars. He welcomes me to the Apache lands and wants to give me a gift to keep me safe and strong. He grabs a long knife from his hip, the type you would skin a hog with, removes his cowboy hat, which has an arrowhead attached to it with some sinew. He cuts off the arrowhead and hands it to me. He says, "I want you to have this, brother, it'll keep you safe." I shake his hand firmly and say, "Thank you so much, that means a lot to me."

The store owner comes out with a big bag of dog food for Rocky and I tell her of this gift. Her Apache husband overhears and says, "Hold that close to you; they never give them away, especially to a white man. I've never heard of that happening." An Apache cutting off his arrowhead on his grandfather's gifted cowboy hat and giving it to a white man, that is special. I am in awe. The Apache people showed me kindness, compassion, and love—it is incredible moments like these that are bringing me back to life.

A village elder tells me a short story about a mountain nearby called Mount Graham, which they call Dzil nchaa si'an, which means "big mountain sitting." Towering at 10,720 feet, it's a very holy and sacred mountain to the Apache. He tells me that their gods live up there, there is holy water that comes out of the mountain, from the mother's breast, and there are particular routes you must take to climb to the top, mentally and geographically. Mount Graham was used for ancient burials, tribal ceremonies and traditions. The medicine man collected herbal plants there and it was one of the last refuges for Geronimo before he surrendered.

He tells me the summit of the mountain was the most sacred where the Gaan lived and come down to cure and to remove evil. I understood Gaan as God, a holy spirit.

Unfortunately, the Forest Service stole the land from the Apache first and then in 1990, the University of Arizona and the Vatican, yup, you read that right, the Vatican, took control and built telescopes at the summit. Essentially defacing their holy place. Neither of them talked with the Apache about taking and destroying their mountain, their holy mountain. Neither of them asked for the Apache people's approval. It is disturbing to think that we, colonizers, would take such a sacred place away from them, after we had already taken so much. This is where their Gaan lives and they did not even consult with them about it. The Apache now must obtain a permit to have a ceremony on "THEIR" sacred mountain. That disgusts me.

It is a beautiful mountain to stare at as it shoots up from the low desert, and imagine the power that they believe is up there. It is quite the sight, soaring so high from the low and arid desert to a lush pine and alpine forest way up high. The history of the Apache is so interesting, and I am amazed by how kind they are as people. They all accepted me, immediately, with hospitality and warmth. I sort of felt like a celebrity on the reservation, and to this day, I keep them in my prayers. They're great, kind people and they're tough.

As I was leaving the reservation, the elder Apache shook my hand, firmly, and he looked into my eyes intently and said, "It will be okay, brother, remember this...It is better to have less thunder in the mouth and more lightning in the hand."

Wow, I repeated that for miles down the road. Less thunder in the mouth and more lightning in the hand. I thought about it. Talk less, do more. Listen. Actions speak louder than words. When I set out on this journey to reclaim my life and break free of the shackles of my panic and depression, I didn't sit around for months saying I was fixing to do this or that. I immediately took action, I had lightning in my hand, I didn't sit in sorrow or self-pity, I fought, I got off the couch, and said enough is enough and I fought back.

Those twenty-four hours on the Apache reservation were so healing to my soul. The tribal song, the embracement, the sunset where I felt so pure, alive, and free, the gift of the arrowhead, the dozens of people who encouraged, prayed, and helped me, and the gentle village elder who made my heart smile. The Apache will always hold a special place in my heart. I carry that arrowhead in my pocket with me to this day. They were such an important part of my healing. They gave me something, as if they lightened my spirit, breathed fire into my heart and shot another arrow into my mental suffering to help destroy it.

I am deeply honored and humbled. Just some white man, riding his bicycle across the country, and this was my experience.

Thank you, Apache Nation, Inde, thank you.

It was Sunday when I rode into Safford. I broke 1,000 miles and only had one flat tire. I decided to take my first rest day to get a new pump and tubes for Rocky's trailer. Rocky and I shared a big plate of ribs for dinner and stared off at the mighty, powerful, and sacred Dził Nchaa Sí'an, or Mount Graham, as we call it.

It was so nice, sleeping in, and waking up not having to ride all day. My body was ready for a rest; however, my mind was still ready to ride. Rocky played with two little kids, a four- and seven-year-old, for hours out front of the motel as I made some phone calls. I had a great talk with Burk Minor with the foundation, a few close friends, and talked to my father for a while. My father was quite emotional after watching the Fox 10 Phoenix interview with his friends back in Phoenix and telling me about it. He was so proud of me, and that's something a son always strives to do.

I went to the print shop to get some more copies of my fundraising flyer that I tended to hand out and post up everywhere. The lady at the counter was taken aback by my journey; she said she was inspired and gave them to me for free. I got all the new fixings for Rocky's trailer; they were also touched by my story at the shop and gave me fifty percent off.

Two people got arrested in the room near mine, and it was time to say goodbye to Jessica. Not a phone call, just sending her something in the mail. How could I choose someone that didn't choose me? I just wish she didn't see me at the worst part of my life, but that's just the way it happened. I've rarely thought about her, but today, resting all day, well, I sure missed her.

It was day nineteen, my first day not riding and instead getting some rest. Sitting there on this lazy but productive day, my mind got the best of me, for a little while. Emotions are beautiful, it's important to feel them, embrace them, and then, ones like sadness you must let go. I picked up a cool, white, neatly shaped, maybe four-pound rock from the Apache lands. I wrote Jessica a note saying "Maybe, you'll find light in it." And, "Sending you my best, keep a smile on that gorgeous face." I knew it was time to let go, in all reality, I didn't blame her for leaving me. It was the best thing for her to do and the best for me. However, she abandoned me when I needed someone the most. I wrote Jessica a postcard almost every single day, but I never sent one of them other than this one. It was therapeutic for me, and now it was time to just let go. I felt the sadness, I blocked her number, and I moved on. I wish things played out differently, maybe if we met at another time, but we didn't. You have to accept things that you can't change, so I did, kissed Rocky on the forehead, said "good boy," and "I don't think you'll ever see Mommy ever again, buddy."

Way past the sunset I kept staring at that mountain, under the big, happy moon lighting up its profile. Imagining ancient times and what it must have been like. Miracles were happening right in front of me. I believe it was because I was truly living in the moment. I was right here, right now; I was present, smiling, and rediscovering joy. After towing Rocky up and over some big mountains, I was hoping someone would help me out again. But, for now it was just Rocky and me on a human-powered journey, on the long, open road.

"May the sun bring you new energy by day, may the moon softly restore you by night. May the rain wash away your worries, may the breeze blow new strength into your being. May you walk gently through the world and know its beauty all the days of your life."

-Apache Blessing

Chapter 8

Into the Flames

NO ONE IS COMING. *No one is going to come kick in your door and rip you off the couch and say, "let's go." No one is going to carry you up that fucking mountain. You have to pick yourself up by the bootstraps and find motivation internally. You must want to be better. Today is your day. Accept the past and move on. Today is your day to become a better you and fight your darndest for that better you. Not only becoming a better you for yourself but becoming a better YOU for the world around you. We all share this special place called Earth, and we live among one another; we need to support, encourage, inspire, and love each other. Not break each other down. Leave this place, leave your community, your day-to-day, your existence, your spirit, leave it better than you found it. Leave more than you take, enhance the world around you. Live with passion and purpose.*

Never stop fighting for a better life.

Never be afraid to start a new beginning.

Always keep fighting for a better YOU.

Never give up on anything and always finish what you start and finish it with strength.

Be compassionate to others, love yourself, and spread kindness to the atmosphere you encompass.

It is with great honor and pride that I call myself a Wildland Firefighter. We hold this position humbly and respectfully. If I met you in a bar and you asked, what do you do? I would simply say that I work for the Bureau of Land Management. I would not say I'm on the Snake River Hotshots. We don't boost or yell off the rooftops; we don't ask for a thank you or to be looked at any differently. We are a unique breed of men and women who will sacrifice our lives to protect lands, communities, and people. Our summers are dedicated to time away from home, choking on smoke, carrying heavy equipment, working with hand tools and chainsaws, sixteen hours a day, fourteen days at a time. We get paid shit, they feed us shit, and we sleep in the shit, and we love it. But the views, friends, assignments, personal growth, the sunsets and beautiful places we get to travel for work make it the best job in the whole darn world.

***

Let me take you back to my first fire season. In 2017, I got a job on an engine crew with the Department of Natural Resources and Conservation in Helena, Montana. I was assigned to Engine 7165; my engine boss was Jay Anderson, and my fellow crew member was Tannin Trafton. I fell in love with this job immediately, as I imagine most rookies do. The amount of pride and purpose you feel is humbling and special, and I love and appreciate a hard day's work.

There was so much to soak in that first season, and I was blessed by the leadership of my engine boss, Jay Anderson. Most of the time, being a rookie, I thought to shut up, listen, and learn. Jay left a door open and encouraged me to question things, to look around, to voice my opinion and never be afraid to ask questions. He taught me how to run a chainsaw, to limb, buck and drop and size up trees. Tannin taught me that engine inside and out, and his dedication, knowledge, and goofiness were ones to admire. We had quite the summer, three men riding around in a fire truck and fighting fires around the Helena Valley. I never was so proud of the job I woke up to and had the privilege to go to every morning. Putting on my greens, tucking in my shirt, lacing up my ten-inch leather boots and throwing on my crew hat and walking into briefing. I never loved getting ready for work like I did with fire.

I remember my first wildfire like it was yesterday. It seemed like we waited years to get that first call of the season and then just like that it comes in and you hear it. "Engine 7165, Fire Desk on Command." "Fire desk, 7165 on Command, go ahead." Gosh, those emotions like a little kid, of excitement, nervousness, curiosity, and anticipation shooting through your veins and body instantly. It was like Christmas morning. That first fire, man, it was that moment I truly fell in love with this job.

It was a small lightning fire, about two acres, or two football fields big. After all that classroom, death by PowerPoint, in-the-field training and lessons—it was remarkable to see it go into action. Anchor, flank, pinch. If you imagine a circle, with the wildfire progressing at the northern top of the circle, we will anchor at what is known as the heel, the bottom of the circle where it started and is typically nearly out. Always, hoping to use hard black to anchor into. Using the bottom of the circle as our anchor point, that's where we start our fight. Led by a saw

- 113 -

line and followed by a hand line, or a trench of sorts. One crew goes clockwise and the other counterclockwise, in so flanking the fire. Then we "pinch" or wrap around the head of the north end of the circle. After that, you clean up the edge, and being on an engine we had a bunch of water. We drowned it out, probably took three or four hours and boy, was that a thrill. As we worked, a big, dead tree fell five feet away from me. I looked at my engine boss and said, "Jay, how come no one yelled 'falling'?" He replied, "Because, no one was cutting that tree. Keep your head up and on a swivel and keep your SA up." Fighting a wildfire is much more complex than the little circle I was painting, but that is the gist of it. Anchor, flank, and pinch.

It was the most purpose I put into an objective; I don't know if I ever sweat that much or worked that hard for a straight three to four hours, but I sure loved it. Most people don't put on long sleeves, pants, big boots, and a heavy pack and go dig in the dirt, in the middle of the summer, next to a fire. We successfully put that fire to bed; what a day. The real beauty I was humbled by was the fact I was way out in the woods, no one was watching, I was doing a job that needed to be done, and I just got it done. We're almost like secret, invisible warriors fighting these monsters. My face covered in ash, sweat dripping off every inch of skin, and everybody coughing through some thick smoke.

On one of the last wildfires I was on, up in Montana, a bigger fire popped off across a ridge from us. I happened to spot it from our fire and called it in to dispatch. That fire ended up blowing up, and unfortunately, we didn't get assigned to it. However, my engine boss was assigned to lead a hotshot crew back on these dirt roads and show them a good access point. As I sat in the truck and he briefed them on the terrain and what he knew of the local area, his hunting grounds...I saw the twenty men and women jump out of their big green trucks, gear up, and they all looked very focused. Quick, professional, and dialed in. I was amazed as they grabbed their saws, tools, fuel, and big boxes of water, and watching them line up and hike into that thick smoke, up that steep-ass mountain, it was such a sight to see. From that moment on, I said that's what I want to do, I want to be one of them, I want to be a hotshot.

Jay Anderson, my first season engine boss, and I are best friends to this day. And Jay, Tannin, and I won Engine of the Year for the DNRC in Helena, Montana for that season. Jay had some true leadership skills that I learned from him, and is one of the hardest-working humans I have worked next to. Later that year, Jay and I left Montana, started our own fundraiser, and went to help people during Hurricane Harvey. We fed over 1,000 suffering people in poverty, door-to-door in the poorest town in Texas.

***

The chances of getting onto a Hotshot crew your second season are very slim, if not zero. Most of the time, you will need a couple years on a hand crew before making that jump. Hotshots is a term established in the Cleveland and Angeles National Forests in Southern California in the 1940s, where they put together the first hotshot crews. They operated on the hottest parts of wildfires, which generated the name "Hotshot" firefighters.

A sad side truth: The government does not call us Wildland Firefighters; our job title is a forestry technician. The government only calls us firefighters when we die. However, our job that we are professionally trained to do, is, pretty simply stated, to fight fire.

Hotshots endure rigorous physical and mental training to prepare for the season. After the first two weeks of Criticals, you become Nationally Available for Incidents. Meaning you can travel anywhere in the country when ordered up. Hotshot crews are made up of twenty to twenty-two people and broken up into two squads. They respond to the largest, highest-priority wildfires and are sent to the hottest, steepest, most dangerous, and inaccessible parts of a wildfire. With chainsaws and hand tools and MREs, a hotshot crew can be self-sufficient for an extended time. Hotshots typically hike into a fire, or are sometimes flown in by helicopters. Hotshots have the most difficult job in fire; however, they also get to do the coolest part of the job more frequently than others, which is burn operations. After I saw those Hotshots hike up that hill, looking so bad-ass as they just disappeared into that smoke, that's all I could think of. I want to be one of them.

I applied for every hotshot crew in the country, but I understood my reality was going to be on an engine crew for at least one more season, and then on a type II hand crew before getting onto a Hotshot Crew. You must respect the process, work hard, and have patience. As a fool, I did not train for a hotshot job, which is intensive, rigorous, and very demanding physical training before the season. Anticipating being on an Engine Crew again, I didn't train with a hotshot mentality instead before the 2018 fire season, I decided to go for a nice and long leisurely bike ride.

In March of 2018, I rode my bicycle from north of San Francisco to the Mexican border, just south of San Diego, and for a total of 750 miles. I immediately fell in love with bike touring, the freedom, challenge, and the ocean sunsets every night.

I loved it so much that right after I finished up in San Diego, I took the train to Los Angeles and then I got on a connecting train all the way to Seattle, Washington. I then rode my bicycle from the Canadian Border to the Mexican Border, down the Pacific Coast Highway. Eighteen hundred miles in twenty-eight days and raised a quick 1,000 dollars for a homeless charity in Seattle.

Two days after I accomplish this feat, my car breaks down and sits in a shop as I am stranded in San Rafael, California, which is a short jog away from the famous San Quentin Prison. My phone rings, and it is a call from Pocatello, Idaho. I pick up. "Hello, this is Kevin." And sure enough, it's Bradley with the Snake River Hotshots. I was shocked. The first thing he asks me to do is the agency standard Physical Training Test and call him right back after with my results.

I wasn't in any form of running shape nor pushup, pullup, or sit-up condition, either. I could ride 2,500 miles in a month and a half, but those muscles did not transition to running or hiking. What I did have was incredible endurance and a strong heart. I was riddled with a no-quit, no-complaining, and strong, positive attitude. I called Bradley back with my results, and he said, "How quickly can you get to Pocatello, Idaho?" I said, "Two days, sir." He offered me a job on the Snake River Hotshots.

Fortunately for me, they had someone drop out last minute and needed to fill a slot immediately, so I got darn lucky, and I was fucking stoked.

I got my dream job, well, the dream job I'd been dreaming of for eight months. I will tell you what, you fucking earn that title, and what an honor to be a United States Hotshot Firefighter. They say you aren't really a Hotshot until you complete the full fire season, and then after a couple thousand hours of hard work, you can now say you are a Hotshot.

The training is very rigorous, grueling, and difficult. We went for a twelve-mile trail run that first week. Every morning, eight a.m. sharp, we were either trail running, hiking with weight, or a mixture with CrossFit. It was the hardest training I have ever done, and I admired the strength we were building as individuals and together as a crew.

Being on a Hotshot crew is when you really see what fighting wildfires is all about. We jumped around, flew around, and fought fires all through the Great Basin my first season. Our first fire assignment was the 416 wildfire near Durango, Colorado, and in some steep terrain. The fire was started by the historic coal-driven train that goes from Silverton to Durango. Embers flew from the train and lit the mountainside on fire. It destroyed 54,000 acres of the San Juan National Forest, and at the time was the sixth largest fire in Colorado history.

I'll never forget carrying a forty-five-pound cubie of water, with my forty-five-pound pack, up the steepest hill I have ever hiked, and without a trail. We saw everything on that fire. It was my first time seeing multiple helicopters assisting us with water buckets and watching all different sizes of planes dropping retardant and water. We went direct, we went indirect, we did some hot line, we set up an epic couple-mile-long hose lays, we protected homes, we prepped for a burn, and we burned. It was a huge learning experience, mentally and physically, and you wouldn't believe the blisters I got on my feet. It was amazing watching the lead saw drop big, hazardous trees and seeing the fire glow on the mountain at night. It was a beautiful, natural disaster and we had front-row seats. I've never slept so well, so hard. It was a difficult job and I loved it.

On one of our last days on the 416 fire, the winds shifted, and the fire changed direction. Coming straight towards us. And we were in big timber. I will never forget thinking in my head, we should get out of here, and moments after that thought, the Supt. came on the radio and said it was time to move. We made a quick hike through the black, down an escape route, through foot-deep ash and thousands of dead, weakened, burned trees. Constantly looking down on your footing but also constantly looking up for a tree that could fall at any moment. Situational awareness is critical in this job and repeated all the time through the day, as is head on a swivel. You do everything with purpose; from the moment you wake up, everything is proficient, and the crew is prepared for any change, any assignment, at any time.

In my couple seasons rolling with the Snake River Hotshots, I became the strongest I had ever been, physically and mentally, in my lifetime. I owe so much to the incredible leadership on Snake River. The Superintendent Randy taught me the true definition of lead by example. He carried cubbies, Jerry Cans, he hiked with us, he dug with us, he ran and physical trained with us, he did what we did, and he was darn good at it. He was the best boss I ever had. Working in such a dangerous environment all summer, you need to trust your leadership, and these guys were so dialed in, I trusted them one hundred percent.

I really became a better person working on Snake River. I learned and grew a huge amount. It's amazing what digging sixteen hours a day for a couple summers will do to a man, building true grit, and damn, if there is not a job I can't do after those two years on a shot crew.

We worked fourteen days on followed by two days off, those days consisting of sixteen-hour shifts. Here is the typical day on a fire assignment:

0600: Wake up, fully dressed, prepared for day in under five minutes.

0605: Drive to fire camp.

0615 – 0700: Eat breakfast, overhead goes to briefing.

0700-0800: Brief on daily mission, go to Fireline:

0800- 2000: Dig line, Saw line. Minimal breaks.

2000: Hike back to trucks.

2045: After Action Report. Debriefing.

2100: Dinner, sharpen saws, tools, and clean trucks.

2200: Bed down.

And, if we were spiking out. Spiking out is when the crew is far from road access, has supplies flown in, and hikes or flies into to the extended site. We would wake up at 0600, eat an MRE and be on the line by 0700, sometimes sooner. Spiking out for two weeks will really show you what you're built of.

Everything was always STC, Subject To Change. On one of my longest shifts, we just finished chow, and were getting into our sleeping bags at 2200. I heard someone yelling my name. I thought I was dreaming. Nope, we got called back to the line to do a critical burn operation. We ended up working over twenty-four hours that day, and I'll tell you, I was the lead burner for part of our all-night burn operation, and that was one of the best nights of my life.

In 2020 I transitioned from the fast pace and intensity of the Hotshot life to a Fire Module in Yosemite National Park. What a dream to call Yosemite home for a summer, and to protect it was a special experience that I will hold close to my heart forever.

The best part of working in Yosemite National Park was when Covid closed the entire park to the general public. Only people who lived in El Portal were allowed in the park, which is where our crew was stationed. That meant that we got to hike some of the world's most magical, beautiful, unreal trails with no one else around. I will never forget sitting next to Yosemite Falls, drinking a beer, and just staring in awe, with my jaw dropped to the ground, all by myself. I made some great friends that season, and I am sure that some of my crew noticed something was wrong with me mentally.

It was the buildup of my mental illness that fire season. I began to have mini-panic attacks, some anxiety, but something about working hard and being in nature 24/7 helped me to stay calm. I lost my cool a few times that season, which is not like me at all. It was the beginning of me losing my mind. I am grateful for everyone in Yosemite that had my back when I finally told the world what I was going through.

And that is where we started this story, at the end of fire season, 2020. When I kissed the granite walls, the most beautiful waterfalls, and my cabin by the Merced River goodbye. That is when my mind got sucked up, chewed up, and spit out into a pit of fire and my brain became nothing but overtaken by mental illness.

This was the birth of the worst year of my life, my hardest uphill battle. After years of being a firefighter and running into the danger as others evacuated, I was prepared to fight this head-on too. It took me awhile to start that fight, but I didn't back down when I began the hardest battle of my lifetime.

The Hotshot Prayer

When I am called to duty, Lord

To fight the roaring blaze,

Please keep me safe and strong

I may be here for days.

Be with my fellow crewmembers,

as we hike up to the top.

Help us cut enough line,

For this blaze to stop.

Let my skills and hands

be firm and quick.

Let me find those safety zones,

as we hit and lick.

For if this day on the line,

I should lose my life,

Lord, bless my Hotshot Crew,

my children and my WIFE.

   - Poem written by Patricia Huston, IHC Wife

Chapter 9

Brotherhood

A huge lesson I have learned on this journey is to simply stop thinking about the what ifs. And to focus on what I am capable of right now. Truly, breathing in the moment and soaking in with what and who is around me. Being grateful for what I have *right now*, where my feet stand and just enjoying **how lucky I am to be alive**. I have my five senses, I can walk, run, ride, hike, swim, jump, dance, and I have amazing freedom in this beautiful country thanks to the people who have fought and died for the citizens who fall under the stripes and the stars. I have friends all over the world, an incredible family, people to call when I feel lonely or to share good news with, and I have support. I could've thought all day about *"what if"* I get hit by a truck, but what ifs aren't reality, they're fantasy. I never said *"what if"* I ride across the entire country; from day one I said *I WILL* RIDE ACROSS THE COUNTRY. Staying present, I never thought about the end goal, how I could focus on the future and the finish line yet remain present to enjoy this journey fully. I witnessed my transformation every second; maybe it wasn't the perfect change, but it was perfect for me.

Somedays, pedaling, I just smile and feel such gratitude, what a gift to ride my bicycle this far.

What I am extremely and internally grateful for, is the brotherhood that lies with wildland firefighters. A bond so tightly knit it can't be shaken, broken, or destroyed. I couldn't believe how many firefighters were helping me along this journey, and the next thousand miles, they came from everywhere to help and be a part of what some said, "Forrest Gump on a bike."

***

After staring at Dzil Nchaa Si An for hours, such a majestic mountain, the sun says goodnight, the moon comes out, lights up the sky and just like that, I get a random call with some support. I get a call from Matt Lister, an old Payson Hotshot, now an assistant on a fuels crew. He is not nearby but puts me in contact with his parents, Tom and Debbie Lister. His dad, Tom, was a retired LEO and raised two hotshot sons. Tom and Debbie were happy to help me. And this is where some true bike magic started happening. This is where I truly saw the power of the fire community step in and support me. This is where I will be forever humbled by the men and women wildland firefighters, their spirit, their hearts, their minds; this is a community of unbreakable energy, a community that has your back, on and off the line. There was some true magic happening on this bicycle ride and I had court-side seats. It was saving my life, and I was learning it was saving others as well.

Tom shows up bright and early, his nice, light blue, button-down shirt tucked into his jeans, a well-kept white beard on his face, and a cowboy hat tilts on his head, a true cowboy. He scoops up Rocky to go play on his ranch all day and I am off.

Around three p.m. I see a big sign in the distance; as I get closer and I can read it, I holler into the abyss, "Yeehawwww!" The sign reads, "NEW MEXICO, WELCOMES YOU" Wow, goodbye, Arizona.

Later in the afternoon, Tom and his wife, Debbie, meet me alongside the road to drop off Rocky. I was just fifteen miles shy of Lordsburg, New Mexico. Just a delightful, happy, helpful couple that I was lucky enough to meet and accept their help.

I tipped over 1,150 miles, and New Mexico gave me quite the welcoming treat. You could see forever; the mountains were way off in the distance and trees seemed nonexistent. A blanket of clouds covered low all the way to the horizon, where they suddenly broke off. I stopped, leaned my bike on the guard rail, let Rocky loose to run around the desert so we could watch this sunset. From 5:13 to 5:36 I witnessed one of the most magnificent sunsets ever, almost like the heavens were telling me, good job, son. The sky above was dark blue and gray, stretching for miles, and way out there, way out where the mountains lay, the sky cracked open and burst into red, dark orange flames and just a sliver of yellow pierced through. It was this vivid red I've never seen before. Like a ninja had a dark red, illuminating samurai sword slicing the fading orange sun into pieces. I just stared in awe. There is something special that happens when you spend sunup to sundown all outside. The full moon rose in the other direction, as the coyotes praised its presence, Rocky making a lot of movement in his trailer as we rode into Lordsburg under the cover of darkness, the moon lighting the road ahead.

Billy Trujillo, the Assistant Fire Management Officer of the Gila National Forest, who lives in Silver City, called me before I bedded down at a campsite in Lordsburg. He said he added me to his prayer list a couple weeks ago and said he had me covered when I came through Silver City, New Mexico. He got a hold of a guy named Alex, a Squad Boss on the Silver City Hotshots, who swung down to Lordsburg the next morning and scooped up Rocky for the day. Alex came in clutch, because between this campground and Silver City was 4,000 feet of vertical climbing. Before Alex showed up, I did an interview via Zoom for CBS in Albuquerque. A guy on the Santa Fe Hotshots saw my story on social media, and his wife, Brittany Bade, was the reporter who contacted me. All credit for this interview is fully with Brittany Bade, and Nexstar Media Inc.

Here is the interview:

NEW MEXICO (KRQE) – A man and his dog are on a cross-country ride raising money for fallen and injured wildland firefighters. Morale is high 1,000 miles into Kevin Conley and his dog Rocky's cross-country bike ride after what was a grueling seven-month-long fire season.

"I started to have severe panic attacks every single day. I felt like I was going to die every day; it was very debilitating. I just went through hell," said Conley.

He spent the last four years on Wildland fire crews. Men and women spend weeks at a time away from their own homes to fight massive fires all across the west. "Everyone's leaving the town and that's when you're riding in through the smoke; it feels like you're doing something greater than yourself," said Conley.

While rewarding, Conley said it is dangerous and draining too. When he realized his own mental health was taking a serious toll, he decided to do something about it. "I knew that I had to do something for myself to become a better person and get my mind in a better place, but I knew I wanted to do it for a greater purpose, and the first person, the first organization I thought of was the Wildland Firefighter Foundation," Conley said.

He is riding across the country in hopes of raising awareness about firefighters' mental health and money for the families of fallen or injured wildland firefighters. "Kevin's route from where he started to all the way to where he's going...he's been passing through places where we've been busy the last several years. It seems like it never slows down," said Burk Minor, who runs the Boise-based foundation.

Minor was in New Mexico earlier this summer when smoke jumper Tim Hart died on the Eicks Fire in Hidalgo County. He says the money Conley raises will go a long way. "Over the years, we've gone a lot further than that into hardships of every kind and sort; mental disorders, cancers, a lot of times these guys will be out fighting fires and their actual home, own home will burn down while they're fighting fires, so, there's been a lot of hardship," Minor said.

Signs of that hardship are seen by Conley on his ride. "I've been riding by all these fire scars and I'm reminded constantly of what's happened and all the lives we've lost. We've lost a lot of lives in fire,"

Conley said. "I think about wildland firefighters current and past, and I try to honor them with every pedal that I make along the way."

Conley and Rocky are making their way through New Mexico and will likely finish their ride in five to six weeks. For more information or to donate to the Wildland Firefighter Foundation, visit wffoundation.org.

***

Alex picked up Rocky and I was off. It was the perfect riding conditions, mid-fifties, patchy, cloudy sky and a quiet road up to Silver City. The first twenty miles were flat, passing giant Yucca, with a swift tailwind, looking over my shoulder a herd of pronghorns ran toward the mountains I came over days ago. It felt like I could see for hundreds of miles to the west.

The ascent comes, my spirits are high, my legs powerful, my focus engaged, and I conquer this mountain. I don't stop, I never stop on a climb, up out of the saddle, sit down, catch my breath, and then stand up again. I stand up for ten minutes straight, determined and strong the entire first 2,000-foot part of the climb. As I reach the top of the main climb, two fighter jets cross above me, making a perfect X with their contrails. X marks the spot; I know I am right where I need to be. This is my strongest day riding, I am fierce, and I am just so fucking happy. I am feeling better mentally, my body is feeling very strong, and the weather is perfect for climbing. I had moments of this feeling on this journey, but today, the whole day, since I woke up and all the way climbing, just hours of a constant smile, a true happiness. It feels so good. I embrace it and I have excitement in my belly. I am going out with firefighters for dinner, and I can't wait for some company.

I cross the Continental Divide at 6,355 feet, the rolling hills are incredible, I am hooting and hollering in excitement. Every hill in front me, I yell at it, "I am the mountain." The climb needs to fear me. I have become such a strong cyclist.

Ten miles outside of Silver City, a cyclist going the opposite direction starts hollering from across the road. He flips a U-turn and sure enough, it's a fellow wildland firefighter, Parker Ashton-Youngs, who works up in Caribou-Targhee. He was on a road trip down to Texas and heard I was near Silver City; he parked his van in town and just started riding in my direction. What a bad-ass surprise. We cruise into town together, the first-time riding with someone, it is a pleasant surprise.

Silver City, known for silver, later copper mining, the birth of our first designated wilderness, the Gila, and for where Billy the Kid committed his first crime, at sixteen, only to shimmy through the jailhouse chimney and escape.

The people are what remain so special to me and what I think of when I think of Silver City, and the face of that was Billy Trujillo. Billy has fought wildfires on engines and hand crews since the late nineties, a man of God and a man of fine character. It was an honor to shake his hand. Billy and his family put me up in a hotel for the night; then when I showered before an interview with the *Silver City Daily Press*, he ran to the store and grabbed me a six-pack of beers. Billy sat in the hotel with me for the interview and said some things too; it was cool to share that.

Then Billy took me out to dinner, where we met Parker, who rode into town with me, Larry Smith, who has also been in fire since the nineties, and Dustin Roper, a local engine captain. It was great. I truly felt like I was with family; well, I reckon I was. We had a feast, well, at least I did, a couple beers, and shared some great stories.

The next morning Billy came and picked up Rocky and the plan was to meet me later that night, up Emory Pass. Which was an incredible help; it was a long roundtrip drive for him, and I couldn't be more grateful for help with the load going up the biggest climb of the Southern Tier.

That day going up Emory Pass was fucking brutal. I had been riding for twenty-one days. After a year of having severe panic attacks that would last the entire day and depression to make things even better, I thought I moved on, but they came knocking today. It was unbelievable escaping and overcoming, fleeing those dark, hopeless feelings. I thought I was better. Back in Arizona, the heat got me; that felt like a panic attack but that was the only time I felt that emotion on this trip. It still didn't mimic what was happening before. As a safety net, I carried a small bottle of whiskey. I don't know what happened today; unfortunately, I had to use that emergency bottle of whiskey.

I had spoken with another guy on the Silver City Hotshots named Josh. He was an avid cyclist, used to race, and offered any help he could provide and wanted to smash a few miles together when I left Silver City. He shared mental health struggles in the past and is a recovering alcoholic who has been sober a few years.

We met in town after breakfast and he gifted me a new, super bright headlight. I felt great, incredible time last night, and excited to ride with Josh this morning. That was all until we turned onto the 152, in Santa Clara. Like a castle of bricks collapsed on my mind and fresh out of the blue skies, I was struck with the worst panic. I tried to tough it out. Josh and I were mostly riding single-file, not chatting the entire time. I battled for a bit in my head and then just said fuck it. I told Josh I needed to sit down for a few, in the shade. I tried to cover up what was happening by using the heat as a reason to take a breather. We sat in the shade, and I sipped away that emergency whiskey. I felt guilty. Josh was sober. I told him all about my mental progress on my journey and then this happened. This happened the one fucking day someone was riding with me. This isn't me, I thought. I just was so sick of this feeling. I hadn't overcome it yet, I might never, I might have this condition forever, but I do know I was figuring out how to manage it. Not today, whiskey and the hardest day of the entire journey, not what I intended, but let's go. After this feeling riddling me for a year, once a month was something I could handle but I wanted to overcome it fully.

Josh rode the first twenty-five miles, 2,100 feet of elevation gain, with me. We stopped at a lone country store at the bottom of a massive hill. It was the last services of the day and where he was fixing to turn around back to Silver City. We had a nice talk; he is a very kind man. I never told Josh how I was really feeling; I just said it was the heat. I was embarrassed.

I sat in the shade, finished my small bottle of whiskey; it wasn't enough to do anything or to help. As he took off, I stayed and tried to calm down for a couple hours on the side of the store. I would've kept drinking, but the store didn't sell alcohol. I was only going another twenty miles or so, but that packed a 4,000-foot climb up to Emory Pass.

With no alcohol, no phone service, I was here alone and ready to battle my mind. I started climbing, my heart racing, my eyesight blurry, felt like I was going to have a seizure, shaking, disorientated, felt like my heart was skipping beats and I was definitely going to die kind of thoughts. My mouth was dry, but I was hydrated with plenty of water and Gatorade. I was sweating and slightly dizzy; it was frightening.

It's just me, my bike, this mountain, and my feelings. I'm forced to fight them, it is hell, but this is why I'm here. To fight them and destroy them.

I thought I was the mountain, I thought I had climbed out of the valley. I hadn't, I was still climbing, I was still healing and today was that test. Out in the middle of nowhere, no escape. It wasn't a good day, but I was a warrior. It's hard to write this…I can see myself, alone, on that, long, hot climb, just miserable. I can feel it. Everything I write in this book is authentic, it is real, and it is true. I will be vulnerable because it's what happened. The truth is, if that country store back there had booze, I would be on my way to getting drunk. I am so glad they didn't because I needed to go through this and cope positively.

There was no hiding, only climbing. It was painful, but I pushed up that fucking mountain and I wasn't looking back. After a couple hours of grunting and grinding up that big climb, I powered through my panic, I endured and faced it, and I finally blasted through it. I overcame it. Holy shit, I overcame it. For all those days I quit half a mile into a run because I couldn't handle the panic, or those times I was so scared and just couldn't cope. Well, today I kept climbing.

As the mountains grew around me, the sun faded over the tall peaks, and just as I lost the sun, I lost my panic. The forest became rich, my thoughts began to relax, and I just smiled. The road up Emory Pass is phenomenal. The windy road curves through a rich pine forest, hardly any traffic, and it feels like you're truly engulfed by nothing but mother nature herself. I took a short snack break before my final push up the pass. I got off my bike and walked among the pinon and juniper woods, only to find a giant ponderosa pine lurking in the shade. I ran up and hugged it. I felt the moment, I felt the calmness, the forest was quiet as now my mind was too.

I got back to my bike, I looked back, way down the mountain from where I had come. Just like my journey started, this day started down in the lonely valley, broken and beaten, and now I was out of the valley and towards the top. I just yelled out through the pines and down into the valley, "I AM THE FUCKING MOUNTAIN, I'M IN CHARGE NOW!" I was gathering more mental fortitude.

I reached the top of Emory Pass, 8,200 feet, nearly 6,000 feet of elevation gain today and 4,000 of those in the last eighteen miles. As the sun said a brief hello again, whispering through the happy forest before it dipped, back again, behind the mountains. I briefly glanced behind me and where I had come earlier that day and decided to leave this mental illness that a doctor called a severe panic disorder and my depression down there, way down that mountain in the valley. I was looking forward.

Legend has it, Geronimo himself stood here with other Apache. Remember Geronimo's last words. I thought about them. He said to his nephew, "I should've never surrendered. I should have fought until I was the last man alive."

I do not compare myself to Geronimo, not in any sense. As an analogy, I thought how I almost surrendered. I came inches from giving up the fight and ending my life. And, now I stood strong, firm, and powerful on the top of Emory Pass. I got back into the fight; I fought as hard as I could to find clarity and peace. Now I had ridden from San Francisco, down the coast, over the mountains, across the desert, over more mountains, across another desert, and up into the Black Mountains and deep into the Gila National Forest. My mind tried to destroy me today, but it didn't. I didn't surrender and I never will again. I will fight until I die.

I AM A WARRIOR.

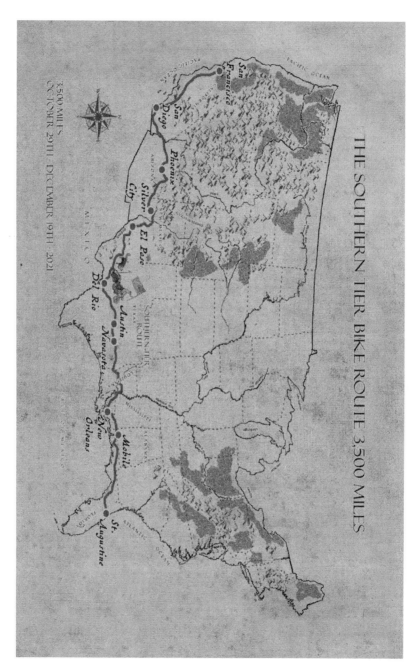

THE SOUTHERN TIER BIKE ROUTE 3,500 MILES

3,500 MILES
OCTOBER 29TH - DECEMBER 19TH 2021

Chapter 10

Paid in Sunsets

Follow through the process. Trust the process. Appreciate the process. Savor the process.

It was freezing up on Emory Pass. I soaked in the moment and decided to drop off the other side to lose some elevation. I flew forty-five miles per hour down the hairpin turns, until my hands went numb. Billy had all my gear and was going to meet me in an hour or so. When I couldn't feel my fingers as I flew down the mountain, I quickly peeled off into a turnout, still high up on the mountain but I was freezing. I didn't hesitate to get warm; I grabbed every stick within a couple arm-reaches and made a fire immediately in the dirt. Quickly grabbing big logs and that fire was ripping enough to keep a school bus of children warm in under ten minutes.

I put my hands near the flames, chugged thirty-two ounces of water, sat in the dirt with a fascinating sunset piercing through the rich, tall forest. What a day of full circle, from suffering to pure euphoric joy, literally and metaphorically from the valley floor to the tops of the mountains.

As I zoned out, full of exhaustion and the beauty around me, I heard the screeching, eerie scream of a cougar across the ridge. I was too tired to care, and, by the fire, honestly, I wasn't afraid. It made a few calls as it strolled up the mountain to the west of me. A few minutes later, on the ridge to my east, I heard a pack of coyotes getting stirred up. The moon was full, and my heart was in its happy place.

Billy Trujillo and Larry Smith pulled up after a while, and in the dark, Rocky flew out of the truck in excitement. These two men of fire were driving three-plus hours roundtrip to make this happen for me. Billy surprised me with some cold drinks. We hugged, laughed, and just like that, they were back off down the mountain. Knowing these two men had my back and were praying for me along this journey meant the world to me. Rocky and I slept by the fire; he'd jump to attention every time the coyotes let off their sweet tunes. He is a loyal dog,

Day 22: Emory Pass to Caballo RV Park. 37 miles.

It was a major descent down the mountain, and it felt like the seasons changed as I dropped in altitude. Hundreds of birds circled high above one of the switchbacks on the road. As I got close, I saw blood in the street, and something, probably a deer, left drag marks in the sand up the hill. Maybe that's what that cougar was up to last night.

As I'm flying down the hill, Rocky has his cute little head way out the window, enjoying the wind and looking all around. It is starting to look like fall; the oak trees are bright yellow and light orange. There is not a single car on the road, until some asshole comes flying down behind me. He starts honking and honking and honking. I turn around and look at him and notice there is not a car coming our direction. I signal him to pass, and he just keep honking. Well, I lose that peaceful moment for a second. He finally passes me after a few minutes of harassing me, and he flicks me off as he flies by. I'm too happy to be mad. I wave and throw up a peace sign and a thumbs-up; good job, you poor boy.

I get down the mountain and into Hillsboro, a one-block kind of town. I park my bike on the side of the only place open, a cute mom-and-pop deli. A sweet and gentle woman hands me a menu. I order two sandwiches, one for now and one for later. I'm worn out from yesterday and chilly from the fast descent. I lie down, resting on my bike, my head on my pannier, Rocky cuddled up under my left arm. I just bask in the bright sun kissing my face and happen to fall asleep.

The waitress gently wakes me up and brings my food out to me. She sees the bike, trailer, and Rocky, and asks what I am doing. Before I respond, I have to tell her that she has the best energy, just something so peaceful about her and in her aura. She smiles and says, "It is Jesus Christ's spirit, he lives in all of us." I tell her what I am doing, why, and where I started. I scarf down the big deli sandwich, drink a couple sodas, and go to pay. And that angel of a lady, well, she bought my lunch.

With my belly full and my mind in a great place, we continued the day. It was just one of those days when it felt the world was still, and you were in your own little wonderland. Every tree I saw, every bird, every blade of grass wisping with the wind, everything just made me smile. I was getting my happy thoughts back; I was becoming truly happy again, I could feel my soul smiling and I embraced it.

As I slowly made my way up a hill, Dustin Roper, the engine captain from dinner last night, happened to drive by. Honked his horn and his crew member and he smiled and said some kind words as they passed me on the road.

On that same hill, a man slows down next to me in a Jeep Grand Cherokee. His wife is in the passenger seat. He leans over and hollers, "Hey, man, aren't you that hotshot riding across the country for the foundation?" I smile. "Yes, sir." He replies, "That is so cool, man, I really respect what you're doing for raising awareness and money for the foundation. I've been with the Forest Service thirty-five years, and I retire in two days."

What a coincidence.

Rocky and I stay at an RV camping spot, near the base of the Caballo Mountains. We go for a long, few-miles walk towards them and down by Caballo Reservoir that the Rio Grande flows into. It was a soft, pastel sunset and we turned in early.

Day 23: Caballo to Leasburg Dam State Park. 50 miles.

Thirty-four degrees this morning, not as cold as Emory Pass when it dropped to twenty degrees last night. I woke up to a text from one of the Apache I had met. Not sure how he got my number, it simply says, "I hear you are in New Mexico this morning. Safe travels, buddy. And remember when you look up at that night sky, you look for that bright star and that is the ancestors looking down on you."

Chili peppers and cotton fields line the open, rural road the entire day. I stop into the famous Sparky's Bar-B-Cue in the town of Hatch. The best damn green chili burger in the world, yeah, I'll agree with their world-famous branding, and that milkshake surely hit the spot too. I talk to the manager, and they allow me to post a couple flyers in their windows.

About ten miles down the road from lunch, a blacked-out Jeep creepily slows down beside me. I'm riding against traffic because there aren't any cars coming, which I love doing, never concerned with a car hitting me from behind. So, they're on my right. It's an odd few moments, until they finally pull over a couple hundred feet in front of me. I am sort of sketched out as I catch up and about to pass them, the back door opens. A Hispanic woman gets out of the car. I can see a baby car seat next to hers. I stop, she comes over and says, "Are you that guy riding across the country?" Before I respond, she starts petting Rocky and says, "Oh my goodness, is this Rocky?" I say, "Yes, ma'am." She says, "We saw your flyer at Sparky's, and we looked all over for you. We figured you would be on this back road. We wanted to give you this..." She hands me a five-dollar bill. This lady, with her husband and infant, drove ten-ish miles the opposite direction of their home, to give me five dollars and tell me they're praying for me. How fucking cool is that? It brings tears to my eyes writing this nine months later. How sweet of that family to do.

That lady probably doesn't have much money. How thoughtful, it was very special to me. It's the little things. This country, the people who live here, it doesn't matter black, white, Hispanic, or Asian, the people I have met on this bike tour are salt of the earth. The poorest of the poor have helped me. I'm just in awe of how wonderful this world is. We see so much bullshit on the news, and all I see is amazing humans every day.

I stop in a big bar and grill for dinner a couple miles down the street from the campground. They let me bring the whole bike and trailer into this nice bar, and all the waitresses love Rocky. There is live music outside. There are fifteen people waiting for beers, and the bartender comes to me first. It's just my lucky day. You want good service, ride a bike 1,200 miles with a really cute dog. Another woman offers to buy me dinner and Rocky some chicken tenders. I say no, thank you. She insists that God sent her to me and I accept. It is a nice time.

Noel calls me, a member of the Smoky Bear Hotshots. He lives on a farm about thirty minutes away and offers to help with Rocky tomorrow.

I pull up into the campground. The gate is closed; I go around it. It's dark and I hear loud music, down the hill, where the campsites are. I decide to stay up here, away from the ruckus, and camp behind this small storage building, in the grass. I don't set up a tent, I almost never do, I just cowboy camp. There is no light pollution, and I could stare at that night sky forever. I count a couple dozen shooting stars as I drift away, dwindling in joy at the beauty up above and the soft sounds of the Rio Grande River below.

Day 24: Leasburg Dam State Park to El Paso, Texas. 63 miles.

Noel, his wife, and two beautiful kids show up in the morning. They are playing at the park as I wheel everything over to his truck. His kids go crazy over Rocky; I express how grateful I am for his and his family's help today. "Happy to do it; my kids love dogs." Noel is a good man. They head off.

I gather up my stuff from behind the shed; as I'm tying my shoes and about to start riding, a State of New Mexico Park Ranger pulls up. He pulls up aggressively; he has a bullet-proof vest on and looking all business. Mind you, I'm right alongside the border of Mexico; LEOs are everywhere. He says twice, sternly, "Did you camp here?" repeating himself before I respond. All my camping gear is in Noel's truck, just one small bag and my bike. I could easily lie but I don't. I say, "Yes, sir, I camped right over there, in the grass." He says, "Well, you can't do that." I explain about the loud party last night; I just wanted some peace up here. I didn't set up a tent or anything and tell him all about my journey and its purpose. He says he respects firefighters, but he doesn't really care. He tells me I have to leave the park immediately, and he reminds me I was kicked out a couple times. He escorts me in his ranger SUV, driving behind me, to the gate and then U-turns. He is not going to affect my day, but he is a dick. I just don't understand why after I say I'm leaving right now and continuing riding to El Paso, he has to keep saying...You have to leave, you're kicked out.

It is a beautiful day for a bike ride.

A few miles shy of El Paso, I see a Texas flag waving in the distance. I stand up and pedal harder. Welcome to Texas. I'll never forget how sweet that feels. Texas is the longest of the eight states on the Southern Tier, and I am stoked to conquer it. I am truly speechless when I hit that Texas state line, what an accomplishment, I think. WELCOME TO FUCKING TEXAS, BABY!

Noel, his wife, his son and daughter took me out to a nice dinner in El Paso. Being firefighters is a bond you can't break, and they surely made me feel like a part of their family.

I took a couple days off in El Paso. It was a unique town. Some say the heart of the Wild West. Years and years ago, the streets were littered with saloons, gambling, brothels, and outlaws, and it was known as the Six Shooter Capital. Legend has it known as the birthplace of the margarita, and Billy the Kid even dressed up as a Texas Ranger once upon a time, and broke his friend out of the local prison.

I got some bizarre text messages of death threats that the police said not to worry about. They even sent them to my family back in Virginia. I did another news interview with KTSM CBS El Paso. And then I did my first interview with Brandon of Anchorpoint Podcast, which I believe went really well and it was great to finally connect. Two police officers were sitting in the hallway of the hotel for two days. I talked to them for a bit and you know what's funny? Only two people the entire ride told me that I was probably going to get hit by a truck and die, a policewoman and a priest.

Leaving El Paso, you hug the border for the next few hundred miles.

After a couple days of rest, I was back on the road. With Rocky and all the weight that comes with his trailer and him, and the miles really slowed down for a couple days. Rocky and I spent Thanksgiving in the world's shittiest motel I have ever seen. The whole place looked like a junkyard, like they gutted every room to renovate ten years ago and never did. We were in what looked like the only habitable room they had to rent for the night. Every other room had broken doors and shattered windows, AC units and televisions thrown all over the place; it seriously looked like a demolition site or possibly the scene from a horror movie. The room was gross, the water in the shower was discolored, there were bugs in the room, it smelled but hell, but it was the only place to stay. I counted my blessings to be thankful for, we watched the parade on television, and I ate two cans of Chef Boyardee Ravioli for dinner and Rocky got some wet dog food. It was a unique Thanksgiving, but so much to be thankful for. I thought back on all the family-filled Thanksgivings back in Virginia growing up. I thought about my mom's stuffing and my father carving the turkey, the kids running around playing catch, one with my grandparents and cousins, and uncles and aunts, so many fond memories happened on Thanksgiving. This one was fond, too; very different but I was thankful to be alive, to be helping myself and helping others, and football was on national television.

Cody Lambert, a task force leader and Wildland Firefighter for over a decade, sent me a message when I was way back in Arizona. He said he worked with the Texas A&M Forest Service, and as an agency "we support you and support what you are doing." He assured me that when I got to Texas, they had my back. Well, he is a man of his word because they truly did.

Texas will always hold a special place in my heart, and when I think of that sweet, southern hospitality and my time there, Cody will come to mind. I called Cody and told him the kind of support I was looking for, which was someone to watch Rocky for a day or two so I could bang out bigger miles. The morning after Thanksgiving, I had a phone message from the fire chief in Sierra Blanca, Texas. Cody got a hold of him, told him my story, and he was happy to help. Fire Chief Manny Rivera came down the mountain and picked up Rocky and the plan was to meet me about eighty miles east in Van Horn.

A few days ago, when I talked to my grandmother, a very religious woman, I jokingly said, "Can you please pray for some tailwinds?" I'd had them ever since. I was forced to ride on the interstate for a while this morning, to get up the mountain pass. It was a great 1,800-foot climb, feeling very refreshed. I blasted through the border checkpoint without stopping and rode a quiet side road, paralleling the interstate for the rest of the day. I squeezed into Van Horn in the dark, under a gentle sprinkle of rain, and met Manny at my motel. With his help that day, he turned what would've been two days with Rocky into one.

Cody then sent one of his boys, Jordan, down to pick Rocky up the next morning in Van Horn and bump him to the next town. I spoke with Cody, and we came up with a better idea. Cody was going to bump Rocky all the way to Del Rio, where my dad was flying into, in a few days. Without Cody's enormous help, my dad would've had to backtrack to meet me.

Cody gets help from Sierra Blanca to Van Horn. Then Van Horn to Alpine. Then someone watches Rocky for two days from Alpine to Sanderson and then we connect in Del Rio. Which allows me to do nearly 400 miles in four days and make it to Del Rio the night before my dad lands. It is a true miracle how this plays out, and Cody, along with his wildland firefighter friends, helping me through Western Texas. Thank you, Cody Lambert, Jordan Petralba, Jeremy Williams, and Jordan Martin. Cody and his boys meet me in Del Rio, take me out to a nice Mexican restaurant and set me up with a hotel for the night. That Texas welcome is pretty amazing; they really make me feel like a brother they hadn't seen in years. I would've loved to have fought fire with these guys!

***

Now, I want to backtrack to when I broke 1,500 miles, the day out of Van Horn and towards Alpine. This was the magical day, a climax, where something in my mind truly shifted.

I wrote this in my journal:

November 27th. 103 miles. 1,807 feet of elevation gain.

This ride wasn't perfect; it was perfectly imperfect but truly too perfect to understand.

Purpose is a determination, a feeling of having a reason for what you do, and intentionality.

Passion is defined by a "strong and barely controllable emotion." I believe purpose and passion come together and were critical in my recovery from mental suffering. I had purpose and I was demonstrating my will power to succeed daily. I had a strong passion to overcome my adversity and to seek clarity and stillness.

Nearly a month ago I wanted to kill myself, now all I want to do is LIVE.

I can't believe the transformation that has happened on this ride; I have truly pedaled to peace.

The battle was hard, and it was a battle only I could fight. I choose to become the warrior and not stand defeated. I choose, I fought, I bled, I cried, I forgave, and I battled, every single day to not stay at the bottom of that mountain, to NOT be that broken glass ball anymore. I chose to fight, it was time, and when I fought over the last 1,500 miles on this bicycle, feeling every emotion, I found myself again. I had rediscovered myself and propelled into a better man in those 1,500 miles, I broke the barrier, and I was becoming the strongest I had been in my entire life, for I now realized "I AM THE MOUNTAIN."

I am raw, pure, dirty, and free. When I ride my bicycle all day long, I extinguish every ounce of energy in my body. I don't ride weak; when I pedal, I fucking pedal. Every day, in and out, six, seven, eight, and nine hours a day I pedal with purpose. On ninety- and one-hundred-mile days, everything and anything goes through your mind. What is helping me let go and is so powerful for my mental journey is this one thing. When I am on a fifty-mile stretch, or today, for example, as seventy miles of highway, with no services, no cell service, I have no distractions and no escape. When my feelings hit me, depression, sadness, panic, anxiety, or whatever strikes...I have nowhere to run, I am forced to battle these emotions and most importantly, to sit with them, to be present with them, to understand them, and as I understand them, I am seeing more clarity and the cloud of depression is opening up, after understanding these negative emotions out here in the middle of nowhere it is time to destroy them, let go of them, and to move on.

For the past 1,500 miles I had been fighting this metaphorical dragon of mental illness. Every day I was taking more and more swipes with my dagger, striking at his ankles, but he was hardly damaged, only to fly off and come back later. But those swipes became stabs and those stabs got harder and deeper, and I was beating this mighty dragon. And today, I pulled out my sword and when that dragon came back, bloody and crippled, and I was going for his fucking head. For today, 1,500 miles away from San Francisco, 1,500 miles pedaling to peace, 1,500 miles of putting all of my energy into knowing myself and overcoming mental illness, TODAY I slaughtered that dragon. I accepted who I was, what I went through, I took a deep breath and I let go. For the first time in a long time, I wholeheartedly felt hope again, I found clarity and peace; for the first time in a long time I was happy, strong, calm, and proud of who I was. This was one of the best days of my life.

Today, there was just something special in the air. The clouds, low and grayish, white, fluffy, and overtaking the entire sky, as if a storm was blowing in. I was bundled up, with gloves, rain jacket, and a beanie to start. The soft, ambient lighting set a unique atmosphere over the long, far-sighted plains, with noticeable mountains bouncing over either of my shoulders, from where it seemed like I could see forever. The desert consisted of tall yellow grass, almost no plants others than patches of yucca, and giant yucca it was. It was seventy miles with no services, and 103 miles from Van Horn to Alpine, Texas. I rode fierce, saw my first two javelinas, almost ran over a giant tarantula, and saw a strange art exhibit of a small stone building that mimics a Prada store, in the middle of nowhere. The chilly weather had me riding hard. I took only one break in those first seventy miles and dominated the last thirty-three. I had become such a strong cyclist; I was now riding forty-to-fifty-mile sections with no breaks. I was becoming an unstoppable force, the ox in front of the plow. I was my own last samurai, surrendering for no one and nothing.

It was eighty-nine miles into this 103-mile day. I pulled over as the sun was setting and I was overcome with emotions.

Even though I still have two thousand miles to go, it's days like this that I never want it to end. This bike trip is changing my life, reviving me, and I am so happy. I went through hell to get here, and I am feeling so great today. It might sound crazy, but this is one of the best days of my life. It feels like I broke through, broke through this imaginary wall in my mind. At the end of this century ride I am so darn happy.

I'm sitting on the top of a hill, overlooking the Glass and Davis mountains, five miles outside of Alpine. I am witnessing one of the most magical things I have ever seen, internally and externally. The sunset has me speechless as it dances and seems to linger forever, throwing out aspen golds and burning orange hues onto the clouds, spiraling a soft and light purple glow around them. It is purely one of the most beautiful sunsets, in such an incredible landscape, that I have ever seen. It brings me to tears; I am moved by this beauty. More importantly, I am struck with clarity, pushed with hope, and raised up with strength and peace. What a joyful moment.

I do not know how to articulate this breakthrough, but I feel better. Today is so special. I feel so much peace and so happy like I just put all this shit behind me, like I am a new man. I went through hell for a fucking year and today is so special. This is such a pure and great feeling, and this sunset fits this moment. I feel like this weight has just been lifted off my shoulders; it's unreal, I feel like I just put it all behind me.

It's just a good day to be alive, brother.

Thanks, Texas.

***

Looking back on this day as I write this sets ease to my emotions, lights a smile on my face, and warms my heart. This was such a pivotal moment in my life; this was the moment I felt better. It was a long, hard, uphill battle to get here, but I got here. I hope this story reminds or shows you that anything you set out to achieve is possible. If you're lost and suffering, you can overcome; you can get better. You have to take the first steps; it is up to you. I rolled off a couch, days after almost ending my life, and rode my bicycle 1,500 miles. No training, no preparing, I just said I am done living like this, it is time to fight back. It was time to get my life, my mindset back on track, to get my mind right and to overcome these terrible feeling in my head. I was done suffering and just drinking my life away; I was done not talking about it, I was done being a quitter and not a warrior, I was done feeling like every day I was going to die and allowing this mental illness to cripple my existence. I was done not being myself and not being happy. I put a fork in that, and after 1,500 miles, I shook it off and let it go. I accepted I was fucked up and I did something about it. Life is hard and that is why we are built so darn tough. They say you have to see the darkness in order to appreciate the light, well, you have to see the light to feel that you don't want to be in that darkness anymore, and that is why you fight to get back into the light.

I hope you learn to love the company you're stuck with forever, yourself. And you fight to get unstuck when you are and you fight every day to feel alive and be a good person, for yourself and those around you.

Believe in yourself.

Only you can figure this out, only you can overcome, only you can devour the freshest and the best of moments. Lead yourself, because in the end, you had it in you the entire time. I hope you see that.

I hope that you never live a life where you can't remember the last time you sat quietly, peacefully, with no distractions and just listened to the natural sounds of the world as the sun set on the horizon.

I hope you can always remember the last day you watched the sun go down, and you waited, you lay on your back and watched the stars pop up one by one, across the dark sky.

As I see a shooting star before bed, I make a wish that others who are suffering can find peace as I have.

Chapter 11

Make Him Proud (Part One)

They say there is no greater love than a father's for his son. My father proved that to be true; he was always there for me, through my rough years, the best years, and now this was the most challenging year of my life and where was he? He was dropping everything in his life, back in Virginia, and flying out to Texas to be with me and become my support team for the next eleven days. I've looked up to my dad my entire life; his character, integrity, strength, compassion, charity, and humor are all of high value. For thirty-five years my father has supported every decision I made. The greatest aspect of him being my father was that he always believed in me. It meant the world to me, knowing my dad believed in me when I set off on this journey. The night I came a hair away from the most selfish act of killing myself, it was my father's voice that came down into my mind and said, "You never give up, son, you never give up."

My father never had a dad. His mother left that deadbeat when my father was just a boy and never spoke about him ever again. We found out a few years ago that his dad, who he never met, was an alcoholic loser. I found his dad's brother, an old man now who talked to us one night. One of the most heartbreaking things I have ever heard was when I asked his dad's brother if the man ever talked about his two boys, my father, and his brother, Bob. On speakerphone with my dad in the room, the old man just said "no." How could you ever be okay with just abandoning the thoughts of your two children, never ever talk about them, try to find them, or even send one letter in forty years?

I remember when I was growing up, vividly, my father telling me time and time again how he wanted to be the father that he never had. He was either my coach or in the stands at every baseball and basketball game I ever played. He taught me how to ride a bike. I'll never forget how many times he pushed me until I finally got it. He taught me the value of helping the less fortunate over and over again, and for standing up for what is right, no matter what. He taught me the purpose of working hard, and patience, and how hard work will pay off. He showed me true love with the way he helps my mother now that she is losing her eyesight and going blind, truly defining love through thick and thin. He taught me hard lessons that I needed, like that one time not bailing me out of jail and kicking me out of the house. He always said I learned by the two-by-four method, the hard way. He showed me tender love when I was suffering and would stay up late as I drank; he would just sit with me, so I wasn't alone, just being there with me. We became best friends when his mother was dying, and our bond has become closer ever since. I will never forget how proud I was to call my dad, my hero, and tell him that I was a Wildland Firefighter.

I can assure my father, over thirty-five years of raising me, after everything I have put him through, he never gave up on me, he always believed in me, he always listened and gave guidance, that father you wanted to be, well, you did better than that, dad, a whole lot better than that. Now, you can look in the mirror and know you were and are the great father you never had.

After the 2020 fire season, when my panic attacks were crippling me and my depression fiercely growing. I had gone home for the holidays, and my parents quickly noticed something was wrong. They saw my drinking. I was so embarrassed about the panic attacks striking me, every fucking day. I felt weak, and just ashamed. One morning, my panic just swallowed my existence, feelings overcoming me as if I was dying, not being able to speak, just so lost, a tornado of negative, never-ending thoughts spiraling in my head. It had been months, growing worse, and I was a turtle in a shell, not exposing it to anyone.

One morning when I was back home, I was struck hard with my panic. I grabbed a bottle of champagne and some orange juice and drank it as fast as I could. It was morning time; I would've loved a cup of coffee, a nice jog, and then go to the gym, but I couldn't calm down. It had been like this for months. My dad looked at me. "What's wrong, son? Why are you drinking so much? It's not even noon. This isn't like you, what about your fire training? Talk to me, man?" I remember holding my head down, I had to tell him something. I was embarrassed so instead of telling the full truth, I told a part of it. I sugarcoated it and said, "I have some bad anxiety and alcohol is the only thing that calms me down. I don't know what to do, but I don't think I can go back to fire feeling like this every day." That held so much pain, knowing I wasn't going back to fire this upcoming season.

I never told my parents that I got suicidal and how dark it really became after the holidays, when I left home and came back west. When we talked on the phone, and they asked, I just said I was fine.

After a year of lying, covering up my mental struggles, I finally told them the truth.

When I called my parents and told them I was in a very dark place and I needed to escape and ride my bicycle across the country, they didn't blink an eye. The first thing my dad said was, "What about Rocky?" They supported that decision, immediately. I spoke with my father every single day of this journey; what a support system to have. I loved telling him the tales of the ride, how I was becoming stronger mentally and physically. How I was finding clarity, and peace and I was healing and overcoming my mental illness. The more I talked about it, the better I became.

Then the day came, my father was in Del Rio, Texas, which the locals say it might as well be Mexico. I grew up with my dad showing me endless Larry Bird and the Celtics basketball videos. There is a famous game in 1991, the playoffs, a decisive Game Five, Larry Bird breaks his cheekbone and has a concussion at the end of the first half. Larry Bird walks off the court with a standing ovation, but everyone knows something is seriously wrong. With that type of injury, he would be off the court for up to six weeks.

In the locker room, Larry Bird says, "I was in a lot of pain, but I could hear the crowd out there and I thought, I can't leave those guys out there all by themselves."

He comes back onto the court, out of the locker room in the third quarter, to finish the game, and the crowd goes bonkers. It's one of the coolest moments in sports history. He leads the Celtics to a victory and the opposing team, the Pacers, were so impressed with his performance after such an injury, they crashed into the Celtics locker room after the game to congratulate him. My dad and I must have watched that game one hundred times as I was a kid. It comes back to what I heard that lonely, dark night—you never give up. Larry Bird's number for the Celtics was 33. It's always been a lucky number for my father and me, and today, the day my father would join me in Del Rio, Texas, well, it was day thirty-three of my bike ride.

I have decided to do something different for this chapter, and hopefully something you'll enjoy as the reader. My father also wrote a Chapter, 13, to give you his point of view, an interesting twist to my memoir and our eleven days together. What I have decided is to implant my day-to-day journal of those eleven days with my dad as my support vehicle.

November 30th, Day 33:

My left knee is messed up, so is my left quad, it's more than a pull, I bet it's torn. Luckily, it only hurts to walk, which I barely could do yesterday, it doesn't hurt to ride, and I ride all day, not walk all day. I got a mission to do, a purpose greater than myself, there is no complaining to be had, just a pain in my stride.

Rocky is playing with a small Hispanic family; the little girl adores him. My dad just pulled in, coming out of an oversized SUV, his blue-collared shirt tucked into his brown corduroy pants. I just got out of the pool, barefoot and tan, it's so nice to see him. We hug for two minutes. He has been up since five a.m., flying out of Virginia, just got over Covid-19, and a three-hour drive from San Antonio airport to Del Rio. My father is in his late 60's, the size of a retired linebacker, a smart, kind smile who has been working in the life insurance, financial advising and retirement planning industry for over 30 years. He has been presented with too many awards to count over the years and raised over a half a million dollars for numerous charities. He has a rare heart to go above and beyond to help others, which I was lucky enough to learn from, and now he is taking off from work to help his boy.

He takes a nap, and I drive, which is a strange feeling after over a month riding at fifteen miles per hour. I get laundry done, take Rocky to an empty field to play fetch, and watch the planes from Laughlin Air Force Base fly over. I just sit in the yellow grass, feel the sunshine, and laugh to myself; I can't believe my Pops is here.

We went to Walmart, bought a cooler, a bunch of Gatorades, waters, Dr. Peppers, apple juice, snacks, and granola bars. I've never had a support vehicle; it's bizarre to think I don't have to carry much, and an ice-cold drink is right around the corner and not forty miles away. We hit a steakhouse buffet, I ate like a guerilla, had a beer, and we both hit the hay early. My father was so pumped, as was I, but he had no idea what was in store.

Every night and every morning I try to think about things I am grateful for. It has helped me heal. As I write this, and my dad snores away, I can't be more grateful than I am. My role model, my hero, my best friend, my dad is right here with me. With a full heart, I am grateful.

December 1st, Day 34:

Sounds like my dad slept well. I put on the sweet sounds of rain and thunder as white noise to overshadow his snoring. I get us some coffee, his decaf, mine regular. He surprises me with gifts when I return. He got me new taillights, super bright ones that you could see from the moon, fresh socks, and a gel seat cover, which is a true game changer to literally save my ass.

Our plan was he would take the mornings slower and relax. Well, relax is tough for my father, he worries a lot when I'm riding all day. Anyway, I would start riding as he took it slow in the mornings. He would then pick up breakfast and catch up with me down the road. We didn't really know what we were doing, just a broad idea. With him bringing me breakfast, I would be able to save time and get to riding right away in the morning and not rely on waiting somewhere for breakfast in town, and it didn't matter if the next town was fifty miles away because my dad could bring me whatever I needed, wherever he caught up to me. Having a support vehicle is a dream, and to have your dad fill that role, well, that is something we will remember forever.

My dad passes me on the road. He calls me and says there is no safe place to pull over, so we meet further up the road in Brackettville. He is stoked to see me pull up safely, and impressed with how fast I got there. And I'm stoked for this big omelet, escaping the heat for a moment, and sitting in the nice air conditioning. It's a strange, little gas station. A prison bus full of illegal immigrants is parked in the corner, four border patrol SUVs and the officers are interrogating a Hispanic young male as helicopters fly overhead. This is a unique sight for my father, but I've been riding by the border for a few hundred miles, and it has become quite familiar.

Thirty miles into a big day, I'm shooting for a hundred.

After breakfast in Brackettville, I told my dad I would meet him at the motel in Leakey and he could do some work on his computer. What I didn't know was there was no cell service between here and there, seventy-five miles. There is a Subway in the gas station in Brackettville, so I asked my dad to grab lunch; I was going to keep on riding, so he could drop it off to me wherever he passed me down the road.

I get back in the saddle, pass a small construction site where I wave to the workers. They all start cheering, waving, and yelling, "Ola amigo!" "Buen trabajo!" About fifteen miles later, my dad passes me and pulls over in a safe spot. I take a quick break, stuff the sandwich in my bag, thank him and tell him how weird this is to have a support vehicle bringing me food, weird as in this is freaking awesome. He heads to the motel, and I keep riding.

This road is incredible, soft hills, no traffic, and a beautiful landscape. It's wide open, vast, a big shoulder to ride in, tall yellow grass covers the hills and fifteen-to-twenty-foot trees are gently sprinkled along the countryside. I see a lonely pronghorn strutting away aside me and a big white tail buck runs along with me, riding for nearly a mile. Sometimes I think the animals understand me when I talk to them. The birds are singing, and the breeze is cooling. As I crest a soft hill, I take a break to demolish that Subway sandwich. As I lie on my back watching the wispy clouds move above, I hear a bicycle chain, shifting up the hill. Lo and behold, two bike tourers, the first I've seen going this direction on the Southern Tier, and surprisingly on a tandem bike. Daniela from Venezuela, and Simon from London. We hit it off right away. They're so sweet and we share tales of the road from San Diego to here, laughing, and it is just nice to meet someone else who shares what I have experienced. You know, you can't truly understand something if you haven't lived it, saw it, felt it, and they have.

Back in the saddle, I try to keep up with them, but they have four legs, and that's a lot of power. They get ahead of me and were going to stay in the next town. I was planning on passing that town and onto the next. Not sure if I will see them again.

I cruise into Campwood, about seventy-five miles into the day. Where I'm hoping to text my dad and let him know I hit this checkpoint and all is good. But there is no cell service. I bounce up the road another mile, now worried that he is worried, because it's later in the day than I expected. Sure enough, my dad is parked right on the side of the road in front of King's Texas Smokehouse. A family-run joint, true Texas style and tradition, all the meats smoked in-house and huge portions. My dad has the grin of a child who stole a cookie; the first thing out of his mouth, as he hands me a hefty tray of food, is, "Holy shit, KC, this is the best barbecue I have ever had; you gotta try this!" It truly is.

My dad told me he didn't get service the entire day, even when he got to Leakey. He got us a nice cabin in the woods and did some work briefly using the Wi-Fi. He said he got worried, just sitting there in the cabin waiting and couldn't sit there anymore, so he drove those twenty-ish miles back to make sure I was all right.

Outside the barbecue joint he suggested I call it a day here; it was getting close to sunset, and he can drive me back in the morning. I said, "No way, Jose. Let's go."

I had a unique burst of energy, adrenaline, fire in my veins. After my father knew what I went through with my mental suffering, it was important to show him who I had become and how I truly rose Above the Ashes. I wanted to make him proud, and what better way than to do what he always said to me growing up, "finish what you start." It was twenty-one more miles to the cabin, packing a 1,500-foot climb. I threw my saddle bag and everything but my bike into his SUV, topped off my water bottles, and hit the road.

My dad was concerned with the low lighting and visibility as the sun was setting. Luckily the road saw little traffic, which put some ease to his mind. As I started to ride off, I looked back at him and said, "Well, this is why you got me the bright taillights, right?"

So, he would pass me, then pull over at the next pull-off and sort off leapfrog me, as I rode and he drove. When I got to the foot of the climb, he tailed me with his hazards on, giving me a safety buffer. I felt like a fucking savage, a monster on this climb. I powered up it like a well-oiled machine at max capacity. A combo of my dad watching me climb this steep hill, up the switchbacks, and the strength I had grown in 1,800 miles, I was riding with authority. I didn't sit down on that bike for the rest of the day, or any part of the climb. I stood up, fierce and powerful. When I got to the top of the hill, the sun was setting, it was glorious in all of its colors. The pinks and oranges crashing together around the clouds, it was a masterpiece as some light purples joined the show; it was perfect. My dad was stopped at the top of the hill, he gave me a huge high-five and said, "Wow, wow, son. That was fucking impressive; I can't believe how strong you are. Holy cow!"

Seeing his excitement and how proud he was gave me the fuel to crank out the last ten miles to Leakey, in record-setting time. I grabbed my helmet out of his SUV, yeah, I don't recommend this, but I rarely wear a helmet. Let me explain; the first reason is I'm on rural, pretty empty roads, most of the time with trucks going about seventy miles per hour, if I get hit, a helmet won't do shit. The other reason is it's hot, I'm a seasoned cyclist, and quite frankly, I just don't want to. Judge as you will; however, I always will wear a helmet downhill, at least big hills, and in cities.

We get to the cabin, in the pitch black, it is hands down the nicest place I've stayed on this entire trip. My dad goes on and on about Rocky and makes me smile when he assures me about my mission and encourages the path I chose to peace. We go out for a feast at the Bears Den; the very small town is littered with the most magnificent Christmas lights everywhere. Before bed my dad reads a part of Tony Dungy's book to me.

Today was a great day. 101 miles. 3,564 feet of elevation gain.

December 2nd, Day 35:

A nice cup of coffee in front of the cabin, it's peaceful, birds singing, and the breeze is gentle through the rich pine forest. My pops loves a plan ahead of time; I always wing it. So we go ahead and book a hotel in Fredericksburg. I hand write the directions, turn by turn, because my dad was concerned about the no cell service incident of yesterday. I ask if he can grab some flyers in Kerrville, later in the afternoon. My bike route is on some back roads, and we are officially in Texas hill country. People think Texas is flat; I can assure you it is not. You feel every slope on a bike; it's easy not to notice or even be aware of when driving. I've heard nothing but great things about Texas Hill Country and I'm very excited to be riding through it.

I drive and pick us up breakfast that morning, fix my first flat tire on my bike, and I'm off. Big breakfast, and I am glad I ate before I started. Because it was a pretty big, exposed, and hot climb this morning. I typically don't eat for the first twenty-five or forty miles. I am dominating climbs now; I stand up nearly the whole climb. I am so strong at this point, so conditioned and determined. I don't slack off; being a hotshot firefighter, riding to raise money for the Wildland Firefighter Foundation, I ride with purpose, and I ride fucking hard. Sweating like a dog in the Texas heat but feeling like an Olympian today in the saddle.

Dad finally catches up with me. It was like a race to see how far I could get before he caught up to me after he left the hotel. It adds some motivation, like a game to play every morning with him here. I can't express how happy it makes me, that big smile I get when his SUV slows down beside me, waves, or Rocky's head is out the window and his ears are flapping in the wind, it's such a cool feeling, very special. It makes me feel like a kid again as he taps the horn two times lightly, and I holler to meet me at the turn for Route 39 in two miles on the right.

Quick stop, for a stretch, Dr. Pepper, and another egg sandwich.

Some strange things out on the road today, other than your typically armadillo, racoon, or deer roadkill. There are these enormous swaths of land, 15,000, 25,000 acres, fenced in, high, fifteen maybe twenty-foot fences. There are these ranches where you can hunt nearly anything under the sun. I'm not going to dive into this very far, because this is not a political story, so take what you choose.

Here is a list of animals you can hunt in Texas, fenced in, for a price ranging from $1,000 all the way to $100,000:

- Zebra, Kangaroo, Oryx, Gemsbok, Eland, Impala, Axis, Addax, Kudu, Springbrook, Wildebeest, Nilgai, Elk, Buffalo/Bison, Gazelle, Ram, Ibex, Simbok, and Sable.

The list goes on and it looks like a darn safari on the side of the road. Didn't recognize some of those names? Neither did I, because they're not from Texas, let alone North America.

It really feels like I'm all alone out here, only saw one or two cars in the last hour and a half. Peaceful and bumpy, as I follow the South Fork of the Guadalupe River. The forest is rich, lush, and alive, the water is calm, empty summer homes scattered around a small lake and a deserted town and huge ranches with American and Texas flags waving proudly on every gate.

Near the town of Hunt is a unique, man-made replica of Stonehenge and Easter Island. It's really cool, fascinating, and it marks the spot where I broke 2,000 miles today. I got an update from Dina with the Wildland Firefighter Foundation that I broke $7,500 with my fundraiser. I'm thinking about all my Wildland Firefighters, this one's for you, almost feels like they here with me sometimes, pushing me, riding with me in spirit.

It's my brother's 28th birthday. I make him a sweet Happy Birthday video at Stonehenge and pound out the last twenty miles to the hotel. I get the perfect wind, at the perfect angle, everything aligns that last push, coasting twenty-five miles per hour uphill as the cirrocumulus clouds cover the sky like a million white parachutes dropping from above, and the sun flickers through the gaps. It was an incredible day in Texas Hill Country, but you know what happens when you put a mountain next to some hills, right? Well, I'm the mountain and I overshadow the hills.

Felt like a beast all day.

Dad made some friends by the pool; he loves sharing my story. We have a couple beers with them; they're a sweet older couple on their wedding anniversary. Dad got Rocky a new leash and a new ball; they're having a blast together. We ordered pizza and some wings to the hotel, watched football, and talked about the day.

It's surreal what I've accomplished in the last month. Two thousand freaking miles. And, even more surreal, lying in this comfy bed, my dad in the other, watching football together. What a magical ride and a grateful day to be alive.

84 miles. 3,482 feet elevation gain.

December 3rd, Day 36:

Regular routine, drinking coffee, looking at today's route and playing fetch with Rocky before the day begins. A lady overhears me talking to a sweet couple about where I'm riding. She says, "I saw you yesterday, on this road, walking your bike." I smile and reply, "I'm sorry miss, ain't no way that was me, I never walk my bike."

I have a very strict rule that I have stayed true with, NEVER walk your bike and I never have.

My dad calls me as I'm riding, he says he was at the Sunset Grill, eating breakfast and sharing my story to the table next to his. My dad is so proud, he has the biggest smile when he tells people what his son is up to, and he's helping raise donations, raise awareness for mental illness at the same time he talks about me riding across the country. Anyway, he says a lady overheard his conversation and was brought to tears and asked for my information. He grabbed a flyer from his SUV and gave it to the lady. She said she was touched by my story and will be donating later today. When my dad went to buy breakfast, the server said that lady that just left bought it for you. My dad couldn't believe the magic that happens on this bike ride, and now he's in the middle of it.

Dad caught up to me about twenty miles into the day. He said Rocky was sound asleep in the back and when he spotted me on the shoulder riding, he didn't say a word as he cruised by going sixty miles per hour. Rocky must have just sensed me, like a Jedi, and popped right up as they passed me. Smart dog.

We met in Stonewall, the birthplace of our thirty-sixth president, Lydon B. Johnson, and at a park named after him. I shoveled down the breakfast he brought; I was starving. Rocky is getting used to having him around; they're becoming best buds.

Two quotes by President LBJ:

"Yesterday is not ours to recover, but tomorrow is our to win or lose."

"I may not know much, but I know chicken shit from chicken salad."

The morning started off overcast, gray and gloomy, quickly afterwards the clouds evaporating and disappearing. The only thing in the sky was the circling of vultures, among a vastness of blue with a big yellow sphere that seemed to point all its rays right onto my face. It was hot, the road was cracked and old, but the traffic was light. The wind stopped, sweat dripped off me like rain on a jacket; it slowed me down. I crossed a creek, dunked my head in the surprisingly cold water, and it refreshed me. I remembered I had places to be. The heat had me lollygagging. I shook it off; it was time to pedal with power again.

I make a turn on a busier country road; I lose the shoulder. For the first time in a while, I'm not comfortable; it's just not safe. My tire goes flat, again, and I pull off into a driveway. I whip out my pump, and as I'm pumping up the tube, the pump cord snaps off. I fiddle with it for twenty minutes; it's totally broken, it's done. I never thought of this, and never met someone who carries two pumps; maybe if you're riding across Egypt, you would. I look up a bike shop on my phone. There is one a few miles away, but it is too dangerous to walk on this road, so I stick my thumb up. Forty-five minutes, exposed to the sun, standing on the hot concrete, and no one stops to help.

Then, a man going the opposite way of me, on a motorcycle, slows down on the other side of the road. He hollers, "You okay, what you need?" I holler back, "My bike pump broke. I can't fix my tire." He hollers back, "I live a few miles down the road, I'll be right back." He sweeps off as a few trucks stall behind him. I question if he will come back. Thirty minutes later, in an oversized, true Texas style, big silver truck, is EW, the man on the motorcycle.

The people of Texas are so kind, defining that Southern hospitality. I throw my bike in the back, we shake hands, and he tells me, "You're in luck, Kevin, my good buddy Shane owns a bike shop right down the road, and what are you doing on this road anyways? It's dangerous on a bicycle." I tell him about my journey, starting all the way in San Francisco, about the Wildland Firefighter Foundation I am raising money for, about my mental illness and my dad and Rocky. He's in awe, and looks at me and says, "I respect that, Kevin, love that story, man." We get to the bike shop and meet his friend who owns it, Shane. Super nice man,

EW tells him all about my journey and I chime in with some more details. He is pumped to tell Shane about what happened, and what I am doing. Shane drops what he was doing, takes one bike off the lift and puts my bike up on the lift. He throws on a new tube, pumps it up, gives a quick tune-up on the shifters, brakes, and cables, cleans and lubes the chain, pretty much a full tune-up in fifteen minutes.

I run out to EW's truck to grab my wallet. When I walk back into the shop, EW has a big smile on his face and Shane hands me a really nice, brand-spanking-new bike pump. He reaches his hand out to shake mine and says, "Kevin, you don't need a wallet here. I'm really proud of what you're doing, keep it up." I share my gratitude, such a very kind thing to do. It's hard to put into words how grateful I feel, but I do my best.

EW was on his way home from work and spent a couple hours of his life helping me. Shane was busy in the shop, getting ready to close, and dropped everything to help me too; they both went above and beyond. It was amazing humans, inspiring Americans like these two that constantly reminded me how beautiful people truly are.

I make it into Austin, where Willie Nelson first retired in the 1970s and where Janis Joplin recorded her first song "What Good Can Drinkin' Do?" in 1962. It's Friday night, the sun is setting over the tall buildings, music is loud, people are partying, the city is so alive. I cross the Colorado River, not the same as the one in Arizona, and make it to our nice hotel downtown. My dad is waiting out front with Rocky, and we head up to the room. My knee hurts, my back hurts, it's hot, I'm dehydrated, and my dad is exhausted.

I'm so used to being alone on this journey, and at the end of the day just lying down for a minute, catching my breath, calm and quiet after riding for hours on out. My dad is hungry, and for some reason I lose my temper, I get frustrated and say something mean to him. He wanted food, after waiting hours for me, and I just wanted to sit down and be quiet for a minute. I walk out of the hotel, down by the river, and just quiet my thoughts down and regroup. I come back to the room, apologize, and say how I'm feeling and hold my self-accountable for what I said. My father respects my words and apology and how I handled it. We order a huge fried chicken, mashed potatoes, and baked bean dinner to the room and bask in the air conditioning. We laugh about the day and about how petty it was for me to get angry. Then we watch a movie and hit the soft cotton beds early on this wild Friday night in Austin, Texas.

88 miles. 5,100 feet of elevation gain.

Chapter 12

Make Him Proud (Part Two)

December 4th, Day 37:

Nothing changes if nothing changes.

Think about that. We look for instant gratification all the time and all around us. We sometimes wonder why something doesn't change when we don't even attempt to make a change. When I was at the lowest part of my existence, I knew nothing would change unless something changes. I knew staying in Salt Lake City, therapy once a week, keep trying new medicine over and over, I knew it wouldn't save me. I knew I had to risk it all, to save it all. And that's surely what I did. Now, after riding 2,000-plus miles, something changed because I changed something.

***

Early morning coffee and a nice walk and fetch with Rocky. Got back to the room and my dad just got out of the shower. He said, "I want to tell you something, son." He said, "I'm really proud of how you handled things with the argument last night. The way you walked away, cooled off, came back, apologized, took responsibility, and expressed your feelings. I can really see a change in you, that you really are working through things and becoming a better man. I'm really proud of you." It was a special moment.

Riding out of the Austin city limits, and it really sinks in. How far is behind me and how little is ahead of me. It gives me goosebumps, thinking back to getting off the train in San Francisco and riding up that big hill, camping in that forest service bathroom on the beach. And now we are here. It's been a hell of a ride, and it's a bittersweet emotion thinking it will be all over soon.

Back to the moment, stay present.

Stratus, low-lying, white and dark gray clouds monitor from above. As traffic lights turn and halt my steady progress, a train blows his horn and an ambulance speeds through the intersection. After some stop-and-go riding, I bust back to the country roads. Awaiting me at a small park in Bastrop, thirty-five miles into the ride, the best support team in the world, my dad and Rocky, have a big breakfast waiting for me.

I'm really feeling in the groove today, just riding with force. Took my first break thirty-five miles in. Now just pulled into Giddings, Texas, another thirty-five miles, and I wonder if they say, "I'm just Gidding you!" I inhale two chili cheese dogs, a dill pickle, a honey bun, two chocolate ice cream bars, and a Gatorade.

Shooting for a hundred-mile day and it's about four o'clock, which gives me another hour and a half to finish the last thirty miles to the hotel in Brenham. After breakfast, earlier today, I told my dad we will just meet at the hotel, you go chill by the pool, and I'll see you tonight. I knew he was tired from the road, and he needed to relax.

As I'm leaving town, I see a sign on the side of the road that reads "William Bill Longley Grave Site" and points down the road. A true Texas outlaw, also known as Rattling Bill, of the late 1800s. It is said that he stood up to any man who stood in his way and was said to have one of the fastest draws in all of Texas, a hot temper, a fondness for liquor, and killed more than thirty-two people. The first time he was hung, the lynching party let off wild shots as they rode off. One bullet hit him in the face and broke a tooth, another nicked Longley's rope that hung him, which caused it to snap, and he walked away freely. A few years later he murdered a man for insulting the virtue of Texas women. He was arrested and sentenced to thirty years in prison, but he escaped. Years later, he was caught again, hung again, but the rope was too long, and he just hit the ground, left standing in front of a large crowd. They fixed the rope, hung him again, and he died seconds later.

The sky opened up, a wide shoulder arrived, and the sunset on the big puffy clouds brought joy to my heart as dry lightning blasted off in the distance. What a beautiful day to ride a bike. I felt so alive, thriving and soaking in the moments with passion and gratitude. It got dark, a dozen or so miles before town. I love riding into town in the dark; I always feel like Batman. A helicopter flew low above, and I got a phone call minutes later from my dad. I picked up enthusiastically. "What's up, Dad, did you see that sunset?" He quickly said, "Oh gee, hallelujah. I just heard a helicopter go over from the hotel and I know you're out there still riding, and I just panicked thinking you got hit; thank God you picked up my call."

- 177 -

I finally make it to the hotel; my dad is hooting and hollering in the parking lot. Rocky is running in circles. It's so cool how they meet me at the end of every day, every night, in such excitement. I tell my dad, "A hundred miles, baby!" And he's high-fiving me and saying how impressed he is that I do this day in and day out. He says he gave the lady at the front desk a flyer for my fundraiser, and she was so shocked by the ride and goal that she gave us twenty-five dollars off the room. She said, "I can't believe you rode all the way from Austin to here." He laughed and corrected her, "No, that was just today; my boy rode all the way from California." She said, "A motorcycle, right?" He smiled. "No, on a bicycle."

We make a resupply at Walmart; Dad spoils Rocky and me. We go out to dinner at a famous Texas steakhouse and seafood restaurant. Before dinner I tell my dad my stupid joke about Gidding, Texas, "You gotta be Gidding me," and we go on for hours with that punchline. We both get a giant steak and loaded baked potato and asparagus; he covers his in shrimp and I get a lobster tail with mine and an order of oysters on the side. When Big Daddy, my father's nickname, is in town, we eat really fucking good!

December 5th, Day 38:

Emily, a Wildland Firefighter with the Texas A&M Forest Service, calls me in the morning. She says they received an email from a task force leader; I'm assuming my boy, Cody Lambert. She tells me that her crew is inspired by my story and touched and loves what I am doing for our fellow brothers and sisters. She was pretty far from where I would be tonight but offers help in any way. I tell her my dad is out here and I appreciate anything ya'll can do. She says she called everyone on her crew, and they all pitched in to help. She says, we want to pay for your hotels the next two nights and get you dinner as well. She sends me a few hundred dollars; I couldn't express my gratitude enough and must have said thank you a dozen times. I tell her a little about the journey so far, what inspired it, and before I started riding, what I went through. I say thank you, thank you so much, again, and as I say bye, Emily says, "I'll see you out on the line."

Mark Twain wrote, "Kindness is the language the deaf can hear and the blind can see." I've been lucky enough to be feeling and sharing a lot of kindness along the journey.

Jessica called at 3:50 a.m. Not calling her back. Too focused.

The front desk lady, Ellie, who discounted our room last night, comes out as I'm leaving. She says, "The world needs more people like you, God bless you, sweetheart."

I feel like a well-oiled machine; I've become a true savage riding this far. I fill up my two water bottles, pull up my bike shorts, squeeze both my tires, front and then back; they're good, I lace up my shoes, a triple-knot kind of day. I take off my shirt and lift my leg over the fork and sit in the saddle of my bicycle. As I turn on some music, I flip my hat backwards and look up at the weather, see it, smell it, feel it. It's sixty-five degrees, dark, low-hanging clouds, and light sprinkles of rain. The rolling hills and wide shoulder make it the perfect conditions for cycling.

As I ride up the first hill, I raise up, standing and pedaling hard to the top. Cresting the small hill, I keep the momentum and fly down the backside, holding speed on the flat, cruising thirty miles per hour and heading up the next hill I crank a gear down but hold speed, slowing down a tad at the top, but roll up and over steadily. My strength, stamina, and endurance are one of true athleticism, my lungs working flawlessly, my legs firm and sturdy, my mind focused and intentional with every movement. Hill after hill after hill, I don't break my stride, my cadence is solid, it's my morning workout, my first big push. The sweat drips off my long, curly hair, fogs up my glasses, so I throw them in my pocket, take a big swig of water, and soar down the next hill. Power, power, power, let's go, push it, baby! I show my character with how I ride, and I ride fierce. Thirty miles fly by and it's time for breakfast.

My spirits are high after crushing thirty miles of nice rollers in a sprinting pace. I roll into Navasota, a small town founded in 1831 as a stagecoach stop. The name derived from Natives' "nabatoto" or muddy water. And you can't roll though Navasota without hearing about Frank Hamer.

After a big fire burned much of the town down in 1865, disaster kept coming and then was hit with a deadly cholera epidemic, and then smacked with the even more dangerous yellow fever—most of the citizens fled. Which left this town wide open for outlaws. It became a lawless town, riddled with gunslingers and thieves, gamblers, and drunks, and in two years the main street was too dangerous to walk down, as one hundred people were killed in that time frame. That is until Frank Hamer rode into town. He beat down, shot down, chased down, locked up, and scared every outlaw in Navasota. Frank Hamer made it a safe place to call home again. Hamer became a senior captain of the Texas Rangers. He led the fight in Texas against the Ku Klux Klan, saved over a dozen African Americans from lynch mobs, hunted down and killed Bonnie and Clyde, was inducted into the Texas Ranger Hall of Fame, and was known as one of the best lawmen of the twentieth century. He was shot in the chest, back, head, and legs and always kept fighting; he died, six years after he retired, of natural causes. He was buried next to his hero, his son Billy, who was a Marine who died on Iwo Jima.

Frank said, "No one kept score but God."

After a quick burger and learning a little about the quaint town from an old man, it is back to the pavement and the beautiful farm country. I've truly fallen in love with Texas Hill Country and I'm sad it's coming to an end soon. It's just so darn peaceful out here.

Fifty-five miles into the day and I see my dad's SUV at an abandoned post office, where he is playing with Rocky in the grass. He lights up, and cheers me on as I roll in. He is impressed by how far I made it before he caught up. I loved this game we played, although I knew he had some emails to work on this morning—I pedaled extra hard to see how far I could get. He's just laughing as he says, "Every minute, every turn, I'm like KC must be here. And, you weren't; I couldn't believe how far you made it. I'm looking down and I'm going sixty miles per hour and thinking how have I not caught up to you yet?"

After a second lunch I tell my dad to just head to the hotel and relax until I call you. The hotel is twenty miles north off my route, so he is fixing to pick me up and then drop me back off where I left tomorrow morning. I start riding through the Sam Houston National Forest; it is quiet, lush, big, tall trees in a dense forest and even though I'm on a road, it feels like I'm riding right through the forest. The lack of traffic soothes me, and I zone out.

I am quickly brought out of my trance as a truck is coming towards me, and one from behind, and my shoulder for riding in—is barely six inches wide. The truck from behind me lays on his horn; I look over my shoulder and he is not slowing down. The truck coming towards me isn't slowing down either. The trucks are going to pass at the same time. I don't have time to bail; by the time I look forward again, I'm pinched on this thin shoulder, with two trucks passing. I clench my jaws, hold steady on the thin line of asphalt before the grass, I hold onto the handlebars tight as I can and hold my breath. I almost get hit. The wind alone from that truck being so close to me nearly makes me crash into his back wheels. I pull over, just to breathe. That was scary. Maybe an inch away that eighteen-wheeler was from running me over.

Back to the peacefulness; the forest is one of the most beautiful scenes I've experienced on this ride. I cross over a lake and a rancher hollers, "good job." A motorcycle gang passes me, the lead rider signals for everyone behind to get in the left lane, opposite of mine. As they pass, they all throw a peace sign or a thumbs-up; the last one pumps his fist and nods with a smile.

I hit a wall; that truck coming inches from blowing me up, well, it still has me jumpy. And I'm hungry. I pull over again and eat every snack in my bag, almost eat the bag too. I calm down.

Then I get back into my stride. I'm pedaling fierce, the road is flat, the weather is cool, darkness is coming quick through the forest and my energy is peaking. I stand up, I stay standing, I stand up for ten miles straight, ripping and cranking. I see my dad pulled up on the side of the road, but I'm in my zone; as I pedal past him, I just wave my arm to keep going and fly by him and Rocky. I bang out four more miles where he flags me down on the dark, forested road. I'm sweating like crazy; he gives me a high-five and hands me an ice-cold Gatorade. Rocky jumps all over me, I give him a kiss, and we head back to the hotel.

We order a huge amount of chicken, every side on the menu, grab a six-pack of Corona and lie in our beds watching the Chiefs-Broncos football game. We bet a hundred dollars on a parlay, we hit, and win $260 before bed.

As I am falling asleep, I think a lot about forgiveness, forgiving myself and others. I had to forgive myself for all I went through; even though I didn't choose to have this mental illness, I forgave myself, accepted it, and let it go. Letting go is a powerful thing to do; it's beautiful when you accomplish it. I've learned better how to accept things as they come and to accept what I do and don't have control over. I learned to give myself and others a second chance, to try to understand people better, to be more empathetic. I've learned to challenge myself on a daily basis, to become better and stronger and adapt to the situation at hand. You learn who you are through a challenge, and that challenge is part of your character. Your character is either built up or torn down; when it's built up you become more powerful from within. When you become more powerful through overcoming challenges, your attitude becomes more positive, and overall, you become a better person by overcoming that challenge. When you go through hard times, you have to change your mindset and your environment. How we act and react through adversity, the pain, the suffering and the hard moments will tell us who we truly are. It's nice to know how you will act when trouble comes your way. I'm proud to know, when my mind tried to rip me apart, tear me away from everything I enjoyed and loved and tricked me into a suicidal state, that I didn't sit there, I did not give up, I laced up my fucking boots and rode.

I hope you never give up and that you always fight. And I hope you help others fight too. We are all one in this world, so we must help one another.

Love. Grow. Learn.
Speak Truth, seek truth, walk light, be light.

Goodnight.

94 miles. 4,200 feet of elevation gain.

December 6th, Day 39:

It rained all night, a torrential downpour, mixed with loud thunder. It was peaceful to sleep through. Rocky wakes me up, licking my face, it's time to go, Dad. I take him out, the normal routine, coffee and fetch, as it drizzles. The rain lets up and I'm off for today's adventure.

I wear my helmet out the gate this morning, wet roads and lumber trucks, you know, safety first. I look back and say goodbye to Texas Hill Country; the roads from here on out are pretty flat, according to my elevation profile. I should be able to crank out some bigger miles and make it home before Christmas.

The roads are wet, but I have a big, safe shoulder to ride in. Traffic consists mainly of eighteen-wheeler lumber trucks and the sky is stuffed with ominous clouds, dark blue, gray, and behind me, over my shoulder, nearly pitch black. I've been blessed with great weather nearly this entire trip, shirt off with nothing too bad other than your typical headwind from time to time. Riding a bicycle in the Pacific Northwest for years, I become one with the rain and never let it stop me from living and doing what I love.

The storm is hunting me down. It starts to rain, light; however, it is cold. I take my shirt off, embrace it, it feels great. That soft, gentle, soothing rain then becomes the thickest rain I have ever ridden through. It's hard to see, puddles on the roadway, overthinking about trucks hydroplaning, gripping my hands tight on the wet handlebars so they don't slip off. Stuck in a sitting position, the wind howls, and the rains seems to hit me in every direction.

There is no quit in this body, no quit in this mind. I keep prevailing through the rough storm. That brutal rain came down for ten miles, or about an hour, on and off, but more or less it was steady. If my dad wasn't a phone call away with dry clothes, I would've played the storm differently. And then I had no choice.

Thunder started to move closer and closer to me, eventually surrounding me. It roared and crept onto my position like a cougar stalking its prey. It was now ready for the kill. It growled and WHAM! Crack! Boom! A lightning bolt struck right over my head, and even with my sunglasses on, it blinded me for a moment. So loud, violent, and jolting. I was soaked to the bone, on a steel frame bicycle; the hair on my arms stood up at attention. It was scary. There weren't many places to hid through the thicket. I came across a small house, with a big carport, a few minutes after the bolt shook me. I rode over and hunkered down; I didn't much care about trespassing. I meant no harm, I just wanted to get out of the rain and thunderstorm for a minute. Lightning kept striking all around me, it was beautiful, but scary. That was the closest I have ever come to being struck; the fierceness is remarkable. I was soaked to the bone and threw my rain jacket on to warm up. I was freezing, I put my gloves on too, and did some pushups and jumping jacks to stay warm.

My dad is my support vehicle, so I call him. No answer. Call again. No answer. Text him. No response. Call him again. No answer. I'm frustrated; I really need him now. Then I remember, I set off on this journey, just Rocky and me. I've always figured it out on my own. So, what do you do? I look up on my maps and there is a gas station two miles away, not far at all. I just got to grin and bear it through the lightning and thick rain.

I leave the carport and ride like a bat out of hell, through the cracks of lightning and the rumbling of the thunder; it's difficult to see, as the rain is coming down so hard. I make it to the gas station, looking like a wet dog, shake it off, throw on all my warm layers and grab a hot cup of coffee and just sit out front. My hands are numb and the warm cup gently puts color back into them.

Finally, my dad calls. I'm a little frustrated. He is very apologetic; he hit the silent button on his phone by accident, but he will be at the gas station in ten minutes, and he has a hot breakfast. Now, let's rewind. Because, in turn, I can't be mad at him. It's interesting sometimes how we shift the blame, when in reality it was all my fault for being in this predicament. Twenty or thirty miles ago when the rain started and you could see the blackened sky looming behind and shuttling my way, my dad caught up with me from the hotel and pulled over. I made a quick stop as he rolled his window down. He said, "Why don't you hop in for a while, take a break, this storm looks pretty bad." I told him, "This ain't nothing, I'm going to keep on riding, I'll see you in a while. Don't you worry about me." Yeah, a parent always knows best, but I'm stubborn. I should've listened then but hey, here we are.

When he gets to the gas station, I jump into his car, turn the heat up, and throw on some more warm, dry clothes. We end up laughing about the situation, how dumb it was, but everything worked out. I get a text from Brandon on the Anchorpoint Podcast, he says your first interview is up and running. So, as we sit in the safety and warmth of my dad's rental, I chow down, and we listen to my first podcast with Brandon.

It is strange listening to myself, my story, and my dad hearing most of what happened for the first time. I have come a long way from where I was a month ago.

I warm up, and power on. The rain persists for another hour or so, then lets off. The clouds blanket the sky, but the storm has passed, and now I'm hunting it. I have two angry dogs try to attack me, one looks a little nastier than the other, and they both chase me. The nastier one, barking loudly, goes to bite my leg as I pedal intentionally; I lift my leg up over the fork and swerve into the road. Luckily no traffic is coming; as he misses my leg, he bites my pannier and rips a small hole in it. Thirty minutes later a group of four dogs chases me, it's pretty intimidating, something about the bike? Dogs just want to chase it, and these are not your daughter's dog, these dogs are mean, protecting farms and cattle. They look like they just want to eat you. As the four dogs pop up from someone's front lawn and hone in on me, I realize I can't out-pedal them. I get off my bike, grab my hatchet, and start yelling at them as they get closer. I would hate to kill a dog, it would be my last move, but I ain't fixing to get ripped to shreds, either. They stop six feet away from me, barking and growling, showing their teeth. I have one hand on my bike, I let it go, I raise my hatchet and yell at them to "get the fuck out of here!" They slowly turn around and walk back home. I walk the bike around the corner and out of their sight and keep pedaling.

My dad and I get a big air horn for boats the next day, which is an incredible tool to scare off dogs the rest of the trip.

I make a turn onto a new country road I deem the road from hell. It's a lumber road, that's what the thicket produces. Big, loud lumber trucks going both ways, a four-inch shoulder consumed with rumble strips. I'm forced to be in the road and it's scary. It will be dead quiet and peaceful, a few birds singing, as I cycle through and then I see or hear the big loud machines roaring down Route 1293. It fucking sucks, for miles and miles. A few times, when trucks are coming from both directions and going to pass at the same time, I am forced to just ride into the grass and hop off the road and let them pass.

Today was just one of those days that was mentally challenging. First the rain, then the heavy rain, then the persistent heavy rain, then the thunder, then the lightning all around me, then the lightning right on top of me, then getting cold, then getting freezing, then my dad not picking up, then more rain, then it lets up, then no more rain, just wet roads, and then I turn onto the highway from hell. The best part about the scary trucks' road was I rode with power and finished the last seventeen miles in forty-five minutes.

Well, I made it. I get through the lumber thicket. It's peaceful again, but my head is still rattled. I make it to Kountze, Texas where donut shops are every other store and my happy thoughts come back. The day is done. I stop at the liquor store and take a couple swigs of whiskey and just sit down out front. Just glad to be done for the day.

We order pizza and wings, watch football, and talk about the wild day. Grateful is an understatement for how it feels to have my father here with me. It's very special, to finish the day and share it with him, over a beer and some pizza. I wouldn't trade it for the world. He is such a champ, being here, supporting this journey, such patience, selflessness, and positive affirmation.

Rocky must know it was a rough day for me, he cuddles up next to me, licks my face for two minutes and makes sure his body is touching mine for the rest of the night.

Spirits are high. I battled the elements and I won.

What a fucking day.

85 miles. 2,100 feet of elevation gain.

December 7th. Day 40:

It's not always about where you're going, but where you are.

I take Rocky out for fetch and a walk, with my morning coffee. I open a few messages.

"Hey man—I'm a fellow firefighter up in Idaho, I just listened to your Anchorpoint Podcast, and it had me in tears. I've recently discovered depression and anxiety the last couple of years and know a few good friends who can relate. I just wanted to thank you from the bottom of my heart for what you are doing, you're saving lives, brother."

"Hey—We don't know each other, but I've been inspired by your journey. I just donated and just wanted to thank you for everything you're doing to raise awareness about mental health and the hidden battles we face. Keep fighting, brother, we are all rooting for you. I'm on a Shot crew up in the PNW, the whole crew is watching, the brotherhood is strong. Be safe."

"Listened to the podcast on my way to central Oregon yesterday to watch my daughter play ball. Super motivating, brother. I needed to hear that in my life in that moment. I told you how I went through a lot of shit in 2020 as well and even into 2021. Where my VA doctor straight told me I was probably going to die. I quit doing everything fun to me. Locked myself up inside and fell off the wagon after over two years of being sober. Your motivation is the extra push I needed, I believe, to get back on track to be the beast I am. No more excuses. I left early yesterday and, on my way to where I was going, I did a hike. Did what makes me happy again. So, thanks, brother! Keep on fuckin' keepin' on! You never know whose life you'll save or touch or teach. Life is beautiful. I also hope I find the courage to share this story to my Instagram soon. We are behind you and hope to meet you someday when you're back on the West Coast. Much love to Rocky too."

It brings tears to my eyes. You never know the impact you have on someone. With just a simple sentence to a stranger, "keep your head up," or asking someone how they're doing, by listening to people, you never know how much you can help someone. I was blown away by the feedback I was receiving from people about my first podcast. Don't be afraid to talk to strangers, ask people how they really are, past the bull shit response of "I'm good." Listen to people. Sit with people. Sit with yourself. Be brave. To be fragile is to be tough. Always believe.

As I sit out front with Rocky, tears fall down my cheeks. I'm touched by the messages from others. As I wipe my eyes, the front desk clerk from the hotel is walking towards me. She has a paper plate, wrapped in tin foil, in her hand. She walks up to me and Rocky, hands me the plate and says, "Honey, you have to leave." I tilt my head. "Why?" She says, "Because you are homeless, and we don't allow homeless people to trespass on the property." I respond, "I'm not homeless." She says, "Some of the people staying at the hotel complained about you sitting out here." A group of four or five people gathered by the entrance of the hotel. I'm in shorts and a long-sleeve shirt; I have long, curly hair. I was sitting on the ground, stretching, with a cup of coffee from their lobby. I'm clean. Is it my crazy hair, or is it because I'm sitting on the ground? Gee wilikers, I've been out here for ten minutes, is it irregular to stretch on the pavement and play with my dog? I say, "I'm in room 314, here is my key." She doesn't apologize, she just shakes her head angrily and says, "Your dog needs to be on a leash," and walks away. The other hotel guests just stare at me. I laugh; it doesn't faze me, doesn't change my mood, just a little shocked. But, after reading those messages, I am in good spirits, and I am on a mission.

"Thou who judges others, will never know thyself."

I go back to the room and suit up. I tell my dad about what just happened, he is shocked, but he says, "It's the hair, son." As we are leaving the hotel, my father has his suitcase in one hand and a flyer of my fundraiser in the other. We pass the front desk, and he hands a flyer to the front desk clerk who said I was homeless and had to leave. As he

- 192 -

hands her the flyer, he simply states, "This is my son, and he's a good man."

My dad loads up in the SUV and I kiss Rocky goodbye. After we confirm our breakfast meetup in thirty miles down the road, as I'm saying bye to my dad, the front desk clerk walks out. She rushes over towards us. She hollers, "Excuse, me sir." I turn around as she approaches. She looks me in the eye; as I look at hers, she says, "I'm so sorry, I am so very sorry. I didn't realize what you were doing. I just read the flyer and it's so inspiring. I can't believe it; you really rode that" pointing to my bike, "all the way from San Francisco and you're a firefighter?" I say, "Yes, ma'am." She continues to apologize. I assure her it's all good, no worries. She says, "We will all be praying for you, my whole family, and I'll share your fundraiser around town. God bless. I'm so sorry."

It is a beautiful day, perfect riding conditions, weather, and roads.

I was interviewed by Andrea with CBS Channel 7 KPLC, in Lake Charles. I felt like I did a solid interview and ended it with, "To all my Wildland Firefighters out there, all my brothers and sisters, this one's for you...And remember, only YOU can prevent forest fires." I rode by the Earl Williams Pump Station and over the Sabine River into Louisiana. I said a heartfelt goodbye to my favorite state on this ride, Texas. God bless Texas, the people, the food, the hills, the country, the heart, thank you. That was the longest state on the southern tier, and it was now behind me.

We are staying at the Coushatta Casino Resort; it is cheap and upscale, a combo common with casinos. We feast like kings, gamble a bit, and I had the nicest shower of my life after winning $200 on the blackjack table.

Bienvenu en Louisiane.

93 miles. 1,850 feet of elevation gain.

December 8th. Day 41:

I roll out of bed; Rocky is anxious to go out and my father is still sleeping. Rocky jumps bed to bed like a little kid; we go out for a short walk and play fetch. My dad is still sleeping so I just whisper to him before I leave; he gives me a high-five and I kiss Rocky. "See you later, buddy."

A cleaning lady for the hotel comes out in a rush as I'm hopping onto my bike. Her smile is warm and she has soft, blue eyes and gentle wrinkles on her face; she looks like a young grandmother. In her embracing, southern Louisiana accent she says, "Oh my Lord, you are the guy that I saw on the news last night...the firefighter riding across the country?" Something about this lady is so sweet, I smile, say, "Yes, ma'am, I'm Kevin," and we shake hands. "I'm Darlene, I'm so excited to meet you. I hope one day to go out west and see those big mountains. I've never been out there. I really admire what you're doing, Kevin. I love our firefighters and I'll be praying for you, every day. You speaking about mental health is so important, thank you." She tears up. I give her a hug and thank her. As I say goodbye to Darlene, she says one last thing: "I can't wait to tell my friends about you, Kevin, and donate. You're a hero and I'll be praying for you, sweetheart."

Up and at it early today, it's overcast, forty degrees and brisk fog swallows the farmlands and peace resonates in my heart as I ride down the soft, quiet, country roads. I pass a prison and appreciate my freedom, then some teepees and appreciate my freedom even more.

I never thought I would be an advocate for mental health and bringing awareness to the subject. Well, I reckon I never thought I would be diagnosed with a severe panic disorder that would spiral me into depression, ruin a happy relationship, waste a year of my life between emergency rooms, bad prescriptions, and self-medicating my days away with alcohol and then come inches from killing myself, either...And here we are. I'm happy, calm, making a difference and thinking with clarity and purpose. I'm driven, my attitude is strong, I'm not afraid anymore and I have healed.

I hope people see and hear my story and never give up and people are there for each other. It's never too early or too late to speak out. You're not alone.

As I ride through the small town of Eunice, I have one of my only bad interactions of the entire journey. An old, beat-up, dented, missing windows Oldsmobile is coming right on my ass. There is two-lane traffic, going both ways, and a suicide lane in the middle; the traffic is thick, and I'm forced to ride in the right lane. Which is legal and the only place to go. It takes a few seconds to go around me, but the driver of this car is an asshole. He is riding my ass, a foot behind me, and then he starts honking. I turn around, five guys in the car. I put my hands up, like where do you want me to go, why are you honking? He sticks his ugly, white face out of the window and starts yelling some mean things to me as he repeatedly taps his horn. I try to be patient and calm but fuck this guy. I slow down, I know, antagonizing. Now, he is really pissed at me. I'm thirty feet from a stoplight, behind a couple cars, stopped with the traffic and he's tapping his horn. For the first time on this trip, I really lose my cool. I turn around and see his friends, who all appear to not want to be a part of what he is doing. I look him in the eye, point at him, and just say, "Fuck you...Chill out!" They turn, I go straight. I shake it off.

I meet my dad and Rocky near Opelousas, down by the bayou, for lunch and we sit by the water. I'm not on the official route of the Southern Tier, by design, and I figure out why this quicker way isn't the official way. After lunch, I thank my dad and tell him I'll see him in Baton Rouge.

I'm riding on U.S. Hwy 190, the traffic is fast and loud, very different from my quiet morning through the farm country. It's a causeway, over the swamp. As I'm jetting down the wide shoulder, making swift progress with a fierce tailwind, I see my dad waving me down as he stands in front of a small grocery store, next to an old ambulance.

On my dad's way to Baton Rouge, he notices the shoulder disappears over a long section of the causeway, a bridge, for miles. The traffic going sixty, seventy miles per hour, there is nowhere for me to go. So, he turned around and came back to this spot. I pull over, and the retired old ambulance is owned by a man named Maurice Davis. He is selling jumbo shrimp, the biggest I have ever seen. My dad's been talking to him for a while, waiting for me. After my dad shared my story with Maurice, when I pull up, he immediately gives me a hug. He says, "The worlds need more people like you; it's people like you who change the world. You don't even know the impact you're having on me right now." He is a hard-working fisherman, a strong believer in God, and he's been selling shrimp right here for countless years. We hug, snap a picture, and I load my bike up in my dad's SUV to cross the sketchy section of shoulder-less causeway. If my dad wasn't here, I don't know what I would've done, turn around?

WAFB, CBS in Baton Rouge wants to interview me and film me coming over the Mississippi River on the famous Huey P. Long Bridge. Huey P. Long was the governor in the 1930s and assassinated a few months before the bridge ever opened. The news thought it would be a great shot, and I thought it was fucking crazy, but what the hell. I tee up at the foot of the bridge. The plan is my father will follow from behind me, with his hazards on, giving me a safety buffer up and over the busy bridge. As I see him coming up the highway, he slows down, but he passes me. I think FUCK! He puts his hazards on, but he is in front of me now, not behind as planned, so it is useless. He got nervous with the fast-moving traffic and couldn't slow down for our plan of action. I wave my hands for him to just go, it's more dangerous him going that slow in front of me. I laugh, but I'm frustrated, and I can imagine he is too.

He calls as I'm climbing up the bridge, slow and steady in the fast three lanes of traffic behind me. I take up the far-right lane. I quickly pick up and say, "Just go, can't talk." I hang up. I ride as hard as I can, to get up and over this dangerous bridge, thinking how stupid it is to even be crossing this bridge on a bicycle.

And then, I reach the top of the climb of the bridge, and I'm taken away by crossing the mighty Mississippi River, the M-I-S-S-I-S-S-I-P-P-I. It throws goosebumps on my skin and satisfaction to my heart as I look over at the river and the orange haze just before sunset. I notice everyone driving, in all three lanes, beside and behind me, are slowing down. I ride hard, but I am baffled by this; it feels like the whole world stopped to watch me ride over the mighty Mississippi. As I hit the high point on the bridge and start descending, I pick up a swift forty-five miles per hour. The news cameras catch me flying down the bridge, and I pull off on the first exit to get onto a safer road. As I peer over my left shoulder, I see a police car with his lights flashing behind me. He follows me, giving me a bunch of room, behind me, up and over the bridge. Like a guardian angel, I smile at him, wave and cross my hands, bow my head trying to sign language "thank you." That was special. I had an unplanned police escort up and over the bridge; he is the reason everyone slowed down, everyone driving by probably thought I was someone special, how mysteriously cool is that.

We stay downtown, in a nice hotel down by the river.

What a day.

101 miles. 1,600 feet of elevation gain.

December 9th. Day 42:

Beautiful morning riding beside the river, boats and bridges and a light drizzle. As I pass Tiger Stadium, and Louisiana State University, it starts to dump. I take cover under a large and full oak tree and toss my rain jacket on.

It's my dad's last day with me, and what a journey we have had together. I just want to spend the night with him, before saying goodbye at the airport tomorrow. The road is flat; I truly miss the hills. I just crank and push all day to get to New Orleans as quick as I can.

We stay downtown and get dinner on the seventeenth floor of the hotel. A guy from Colombia has a pop-up restaurant with authentic Colombian food. We chow down, drink a few beers, and laugh as we reminisce on our time together. We are both in shock; we crossed the entire state of Texas and made it all the way to New Orleans. It's a bittersweet, being the last night with my dad.

We go to Dave and Busters, play games, and just have a wonderful time together.

I drive my dad to the airport the next morning, give him the biggest hug and express my greatest gratitude to him and how meaningful it was to have him with me. I can't express how special that was. As he pulls up his mask in the airport, he starts crying, and says, "I'm so proud of you, son." I watch him walk away; tears start to come down my face. I'm so lucky to have a father like him; I'm so lucky and grateful to call him my dad.

I hope whoever you are, reading this, you hold your family tight and close. You only have one family, your time is not guaranteed, so make the most of it. Forgive each other, listen to each other, love and support each other, don't hesitate to call or visit your family and always tell them you love them and most of all, have fun together.

You have one very special life, make the most of it. Make your time on this planet count, make those around you better, and spend time with quality people.

I love you Mom and Dad, and my little brother, John. Oh, so much.

This chapter is dedicated to Daniel Laird, a helicopter captain from the Tahoe National Forest. He served twenty years with the United States Forest Service. He died in a helicopter crash in the Sam Houston National Forest, assisting on a controlled burn. I rode close by the accident.

Rest In Peace, Daniel.

Chapter 13

The Bond Grows Stronger

(This chapter is written by my father, Kevin Sr., from his point of view of our time together.)

As the flight attendant announces our landing at San Antonio International Airport in Texas, anticipation is running through my mind. How is KC doing? He seemed to be struggling at Christmas time when I had seen him. He drank a lot and didn't quite seem himself. My conversations with him by phone were tough some days. He seemed distant and unhappy. Would I arrive in Del Rio to see an enlightened, strong, energetic, and positive young man again? We had talked about faith for the first time in many years. I pray for him daily and always ask God to keep him safe and strong. As we flew over the airport, I thought of forty years earlier passing through my mind. I had gone through Basic Training in 1977 for the US Air Force, 3202 Squadron, Flight 486, Honor Flight with Sgt. Gonzalez as our drill sergeant. Tough six weeks but I actually loved the challenge. Now KC was facing the challenge of a lifetime. Could he turn his life around? Would he rally like he always does with a physical challenge?

I rented a car and headed to Del Rio. A four-hour drive across the plains of Texas. First stop, Whataburger. Best pattie melt sandwich ever. As I drove along, thoughts crossed through my mind of KC's childhood, teen years, marijuana and alcohol problems, recovery programs, orange jumpsuits, courtrooms, and on and on. But thanks be to God, he emerged, hiking the Appalachian Trail, the Pacific Crest Trail (raising money for inner-city kids), building a t-shirt company called Backcountry Ninjas, helping thousands of homeless people in Seattle, biking from Canada to Mexico, helping the hurricane victims in Houston, and on and on. He had become a man. He had become someone that cared about others. He spread love and kindness. Though not perfect, he was an all-around good guy, loving son, grandson, and brother.

As I close in on Del Rio, Texas, it gets ugly. The terrain is rough, as tumbleweeds rolling across the road, and the town seems rough too. Dirty, dusty, and rundown. It is a border town to Mexico and appears to be third world. The navigation system in the big SUV I had rented in San Antonio is spot on and gets me to the motel. I spot KC and his dog, Rocky, as I pull into the courtyard. Lots of pickup trucks and sketchy-looking people around, but seeing KC's huge smile and welcoming arms makes it all worthwhile. His hug about breaks my ribs but I welcome it. I had experienced Covid ten days before but was feeling strong. We go to dinner and catch up a bit and he seems strong and confident. We head over to the Walmart and buy a cooler, Gatorade, and other supplies. He is a very experienced hiker and biker and knows all there is to know about safety and how to get from point A to point B and survive along the way. He knows how to stop and smell the roses better than most and enjoys sunsets after a long day's bike ride.

The next morning, we get up relatively early. He has a routine, with coffee and walking his dog, Rocky. I stay out of the way. He hits the road and asks me to meet him with breakfast at Brackettville. I go to a local breakfast café. Classic Texas undertones and I love it. I order a huge to-go order of pancakes, scrambled eggs, toast, and hash browns. A veritable feast for my boy after he bangs out thirty-five miles by 10:30 a.m. Brackettville is a four-way intersection in the Texas prairie. A gas station, with a Subway and a lot of interesting traffic. I walk Rocky with a leash, which he is not happy about. KC lets him run free, but I am concerned for his safety, so I keep him reeled in. He looks up at me from time to time trying to figure things out. I wonder what he is thinking. Does he understand KC's struggle with mental health? He seems to understand, and I believe he has been a worthy companion for him. As I wait, two buses pull up with illegal immigrants on board being brought back to Mexico. Mexican guards get off the bus as it gets refueled. Moments later a Border Patrol car shows up and then another as they approach a young man sitting by the Subway shop. KC arrives after biking thirty-five miles looking sweaty but energetic. "Howdy, dad." I hand him a Gatorade from the cooler, so he hits that first. I pull out his breakfast and he wolfs it down. He is loving the syrup and butter as it spills off the pancakes with every bite. He hits the bathroom, shows me the route to follow, and says see ya.

Today we are biking from Del Rio to Leakey. A hundred-mile day in the desert heat, open plains and concerns of cartels, illegal immigrants, and pickup trucks with tinted windows and gun racks. My job is to get to Leakey and establish a beachhead. Meaning get a hotel and scout out the town. As I head across this open country, with tumbleweed blowing across the road and the sunbaking the asphalt, I try to imagine the inner strength that my boy had to have had to get this far. He started over a month earlier, as a lost soul, but now has rallied and seems to be finding a purpose.

I set up our hotel in this tiny town of 200 people, in some foothills after the plains. My last twenty miles are uphill and I think to myself, how the heck will KC be able to do this after already riding eighty miles? I fuel up and as I discovered earlier, I have no cell coverage. No navigation system and no maps. I find a small hotel with cabins and book us for the night.

I walk Rocky and we head back down the road to find KC. I drive for thirty miles in the extreme heat before I see KC on the horizon. It was scary every day when I ran escort for him, scouted roads, and watched the weather. I finally get to him, and we meet eighty miles in at a hole-in-the-wall barbeque joint. Best Barbeque Sandwich ever. KC chows down on two BBQ sandwiches, some cole slaw and a Dr. Pepper. He's off again. I said, "KC, the last twenty are uphill and it may be smarter to stop here and start fresh in the a.m." He smiles and says confidently, "I've got this, Dad!" As darkness settles in after sunset, I decide I will ride escort the rest of the way in. I put on my flashers and follow him. He pedals mile after mile up the hills and s-curves, never stopping. He stands up practically the whole way. He finally gets to the top after two hours of relentless pedaling. This guy is a Beast. A bicycling machine. His determination is remarkable. As I ride shotgun behind him, the traffic is thin. I start to video his progress and tenacity. I flash back to his youth. Whatever the sport, whatever the challenge he would get an incredibly determined look on his face. He looked at me and would say, "I've got this, Dad"! He would practice free-throw shooting for hours for basketball. He would practice pitching until he got the fastball truly humming. He ran a five-mile race at nine years old without any training and won his age group.

As we breach the top of the mountain and I follow him into Leakey, we come upon the most beautiful Christmas decorations on trees and signs with lights everywhere. Almost like welcoming KC to town. Rocky practically leaps from the car window to get to KC as he pulls up beside the SUV at the end of his ride. Rocky adores KC and still can't figure out who I am.

The next day it is on to Fredericksburg, Texas. It is a classic old town with very cool bars, saloons, restaurants, and a bike shop. It was established 150 years earlier by Polish and German settlers. My new routine is to go get breakfast for KC and meet him thirty-five miles down the road. After breakfast I speak with the waitress and tell her of KC's journey and motivation. She says, wait a minute I have something for you and KC. She comes back with a beautiful prayer card that encourages faith and hope and she says, "God bless your boy."

I establish a beachhead at a Best Western and head over to the town bike shop where KC has asked me to buy a new bike tire, tube, and some other supplies. I give them brochures about KC's bike ride across the country to post and promote the fundraiser he is doing for mental health and the Wildland Firefighter Foundation. Firefighters have been awesome at supporting KC's bike trip. Some have joined him to ride for thirty miles side by side, some have bought him hotel rooms and meals, and others have greeted him and made sure he was safe crossing their county or part of the country. It brings me to tears seeing how tight the wildland firefighter community truly is, after hearing KC tell me about them. They have had his back the whole way. All they know is that KC is one of them. He is a Hotshot and they respect that. If he is biking across the country to raise money and awareness for their fallen brethren, then that's all they need to know. I remember driving for mile after mile and thinking how lonely and tough it must be for KC to cover all this terrain. He texted me that he was on the outskirts of town and had a flat. Rocky and I poured into the SUV and headed out. Rocky and I had spent the afternoon throwing his ball and playing retrieve. He is a smart dog. I had gone to Walgreens to buy him a new leash and ball that day. Funniest thing. Every time I lock the car and go into a store or hotel or whatever, the alarm goes off. The SUV is set up with an alarm for kids, so you don't leave them in the car. His weight is just enough to set off the alarm. Laughable now but a pain in the butt when I was trying to accomplish things like get more Gatorade and supplies and the alarm would go off.

We find KC at a gas station near a big intersection where his tire gave out. Fortunately, we have everything he needs to fix it back at the hotel room. We work out a new technique with an online video for changing tires that night. The next morning, I bring KC back to where he got his flat tire last night, and he is off riding early. I go to a nearby breakfast joint. As I'm sitting there, I talk up a young couple and we chat about what he is doing to raise money for firefighters. I mention his mental health struggles with panic and anxiety attacks and depression, and they listen intently. I go out to the car for some brochures and everyone sitting around my table asks for one. This older lady to my left looks over at me and says, "What your son is doing is admirable. I'm sorry

I eavesdropped on your conversation but what he is doing is so important." She is in tears when she says these words. Next thing I know is she has paid for my breakfast and the big to-go order for KC. She asks for a brochure and says she will be donating on the site that day. Little did I know that this experience would duplicate itself over and over on the trip. KC was indeed making a difference in the world and people loved it. With all the crap going on in the world, this one little thing was a speck of hope for them. A message of humanity doing good for others.

KC had been on the news in Phoenix, Albuquerque, and different towns in Texas. People began to recognize him as the firefighter guy with the dog named Rocky. They never forgot Rocky. The next stop was Austin. We stopped at President Lyndon Johnson's hometown. I took Rocky for a walk in a cool park and KC came rolling up as usual for his mid

day refuel of food and Gatorade or soda. We stayed at the Holiday Inn by the river. He got in later than expected because another bike issue. He got help from a guy on a motorcycle who knew a guy who owned a bike shop and they totally set him up. When they heard the story of him riding for the firefighters, they paid for all his repairs.

This kind of generosity followed us everywhere across this great country. Americans truly are the best people in the world. The next day we head to Brenham, Texas. Another smallish town but with a lot of restaurants and stores. We stay at the Baymont Hotel. Nicest rooms so far. Rocky and I play ball and go for a long walk. KC rides into the dark. It makes me nervous when he does this, but he is trying to bike 850 miles while I am there to escort him and care for Rocky so I understand. We sit out front for several hours not sure when he will arrive. A medivac helicopter flies over the highway where I know he is biking, and I begin to pray. Please, dear God, keep KC safe and strong. My prayers are answered as he arrives at 7:45 p.m. It was a dangerous highway and though I had bought him a super powerful taillight, I was still very tense and nervous. As I sit and wonder how he is doing, it reminds me of the many nights when he was a troubled teen when he would sneak out of the house, sell marijuana, get arrested, and I'd have to hire an attorney to try to help him work his way through his most recent indiscretion. We sent him to therapeutic boarding schools and programs designed to help him turn his life around so he didn't have to go to jail. We loved him so much and hated not having him at home, but it was the right thing to do. We had three visits to juvenile detention centers and several times when he went to adult detention centers in his early twenties. It broke my heart seeing him in a bright orange jumpsuit, knowing his potential and who he truly was, I will never forget the look of shame and disappointment on his face. The good news is this time when I saw his smile and look as he caught sight of me, he was a changed man. And, all those days were a lifetime behind us. He was a good guy, doing good things. He was a son that makes me proud every day now.

Next stop is Hyattsville, Texas. We stay at a Hampton Inn off a main road. I go and meet KC as darkness is setting in. We eat in the room that night after ordering food to be delivered. He goes out in the a.m. as per his usual routine with Rocky and his coffee. As he is sitting out front of the hotel, the manager comes out with a plate of food and says you cannot stay here. She thinks he is homeless. Other patrons have pointed him out as being a homeless guy. Grant it, KC, with his long hair, beard, and mustache along with dirty bike pants, etc., does look slightly homeless, but this is out of line. He explains he is staying at the hotel. I come down with Rocky to leave and give the lady at the front desk a brochure, showing that he is a firefighter biking across the country to raise awareness and money for the Wildland Firefighter Foundation. I say, by the way, the homeless guy is my son. She is mortified. Gets coffee for KC and is very embarrassed.

KC heads off to Lumberton, our next stop on our journey. My oil change light has been going off for hundreds of miles. It starts with, "You may need to change your oil soon," the next day it is, "Oil change is essential," the next day, "Oil change is essential, or the car may not work anymore." I am paying attention to the weather this a.m. as it is cloudy, and thunderstorms are in the area. About 11:00 a.m. KC texts me that he is concerned so I catch up with him and offer a ride. He says, no I want to keep going. Finally, all heck breaks loose as I'm getting donuts at a drive-thru donut shop (best donuts ever). I speed back to his location and thunder and lightning are crashing all around. He gets to the gas station a few minutes before I arrive.

KC says, "That was crazy, Dad." He sits in the car with me for an hour as the storm passes. We listen to a podcast he was doing with a friend of his about mental illness and firefighters. It is pretty emotional. It is obvious to me that KC was not in a good place when he did that first podcast. He ultimately did two others during his journey, and you could see the light of hope, happiness, and joy coming through in his voice and attitude. He was KC again, spreading positivity and kindness. He rides into the darkness again that night and I pick him up ten miles past town. Dark country roads that scare the crap out of me. We have a feast of fried chicken better than you can ever imagine in the room that night. I had gotten more brochures printed up at the local Staples and hand them out at Starbucks, etc., that afternoon. It rains the next morning, so I bring the car to get the much-needed oil change. I give out brochures to the mechanics at the Jiffy Lube and one of them says his dad was a firefighter. Pretty common to have people have some connection to firefighters, or first responders in this country and it garners great respect.

Kinder is the next town on our ride for the day. A small town off a country road with several large casinos as we have crossed into Louisiana. KC and I dine on the best gumbo soup, po' boy shrimp sub and a lobster for KC. He earned it. The next morning, he heads out early and as I'm leaving the hotel, the maid comes out and says, "Sir, is the young man the firefighter your son?" She has a strong southern drawl and is all fired up. She says, "That's Rocky with you, isn't it?" She says, "I saw your boy on the news last night. God bless him for what he is doing. We need people like him doing good things. The country needs your boy right now." I say, "Yes, this is Rocky, and thank you for your kind words." She says one more thing again. "God bless him, sir, God bless him." Needless to say, I got in the car, and it hit me hard with tears. That's my son, making a difference out there.

What KC is doing is something very special for average Americans. As I drive to Baton Rouge, many thoughts begin to flow through my head. I remember times at our beach place in Duck, NC when

KC would run up out of the surf and sit on my lap soaking wet and I'd hold him and we'd sit for an hour and look out at the waves, wondering what the future would bring. I thought to myself right at that moment that even though I was not the perfect dad, I did my best. Even though KC's childhood was not perfect, he had turned out to be one heck of a guy. He was making a difference in people's lives in a big way. He was on the news in Port Charles and then the following night in Baton Rouge.

I am driving ahead and realize as I cross a dangerous spillway there is no place for a bike rider. Two lanes, side by side, at sixty miles an hour and no shoulder. So, I circle back and wait for KC. As I wait before this bridge, a man with an old, beat-up ambulance pulls up. He is an African American in his late sixties, like me. He is selling jumbo shrimp. So, I walk up to him and introduce myself and ask him a question. Are these really jumbo shrimp in that cooler? He opens the cooler and yes indeed, these are the real thing. Nine-inch-long jumbo shrimp. We chat for a moment about KC's bike ride across the country to raise awareness and money for firefighters and then KC arrives. He tells KC not to ride across the spillway. He says it is too dangerous. He is Cajun and has a strong accent. He introduces himself to KC. He then randomly hugs KC and says, "May God bless your journey." Another amazing American. Rocky and I are good friends by now. I feed him treats and take him for walks and throw the ball for him endlessly. KC is having TV coverage by ABC in Baton Rouge. They want him to come across a well-trafficked bridge into town so they can film him. Super dangerous. I botch the escort. I am supposed to ride behind KC but as we approach the bridge with traffic going sixty miles an hour in two lanes, I get ahead of him. He is now on his own. I try to circle back but it is too late. KC makes it with a God-sent, magical and spontaneous police escort that shows up out of nowhere. The newsman meets us at the Holiday Inn overlooking the Mississippi River. He does an interview with KC in the lobby while the vacuum cleaner is running full steam ahead in a nearby room. KC has become a good interview for reporters as he has become more and more professional, speaking clearly and articulating his mission to help firefighters' families.

The next day we head to New Orleans. We spend a nice night together going to Dave and Busters and playing all kinds of games - like we did for KC's birthdays as a youth. We have some dinner at the seventeenth-floor sky lounge and roof bar. This is a pretty nice hotel compared to where we have been. Nice shower and comfortable beds. The next morning the routine has changed. KC is taking a rest day. I am exhausted after eleven days. Pretty funny, he rode 850 miles and I'm the one who is pooped. I say goodbye to Rocky and KC escorts me to the airport. He makes sure I am safe and catch my plane on time and then heads off to finish his journey.

As I sit waiting for my plane at my gate, happy thoughts flow through my mind. KC was a superstar biker. Never gives up and never gives in. We have had good talks and understand each other better than ever. His future is bright, and he has a purpose. I am leaving him very confident that he will complete this journey to St. Augustine. Three thousand five hundred miles across this great country. His spirit is very much alive again. He is reborn. I have great faith in God and believe he has put my son with me and on this earth for a reason. As he grows through his life's journey, he is learning more and more what that reason is. He is pedaling for peace, and after witnessing this firsthand - I am at peace too.

Chapter 14

Two More Chains

The darkness tried to abolish my light

Not knowingly the light was too powerful to ever forget

The darkness was fragile and unbearable, but it was only a façade against what was real

It was temporarily blinding

However, the light was too truthful to be forgotten and the darkness I just simply got lost in

The light was constant and so powerful, that the darkness stood no chance

But I had to want the light more than to accept and agree with the darkness

The light was a choice, the darkness was a fault

The darkness had engulfed and swallowed me, I couldn't find the light

Until I realized I didn't need the light, for I had the light within me the entire time

I just had to let it shine, for I looked at myself and realized...

I was the light the entire time.

Healing is defined as the process of making or becoming sound or healthy again. I was renewed; I had my zest for life fully resurrected. I escaped the spider web that depression held me in and flew away so peacefully. I overcame my depression, panic disorder, and suicidal thoughts—it took a long time, but I retaught my brain how to work and I healed and became sound and healthy again. After healing I still had some work to do, and now it is time to finish this journey strong.

From New Orleans, I only had three of the eight states left to go. Mississippi, Alabama, and Florida. It was only 700 miles that separated me from my goal of riding coast to coast and finishing in St. Augustine, Florida.

Damn, I am torn. Part of me is happy to be alone again. However, the greater part of me already misses my father. What a guy, what an experience we shared, a memory we will hold onto forever. He got to be a part of the biggest transformation of my entire life. He got to witness me at my best and an all-time high, living with a greater purpose and witnessing the miracles happening around us every day. I got used to having him around, as did Rocky, and it hit me with some sadness when he wasn't there this morning. You can tell how much someone truly means to you by how you feel when they aren't with you, and how you miss their presence.

I scooped up Rocky and we went for a walk around the giant skyscrapers, the home of Mardi Gras, where Arlo Guthrie took the train

"The City of New Orleans," and Louis "Satchmo" Armstrong took jazz from the streets and clubs on to show the world it was a true art.

With Rocky enjoying all the attention, we swung into the Pythian Market to grab a mimosa at Bar 1908. I could hardly walk, the pain in my knees and quads was nearly unbearable. I decided to take a day off before my final push. As I ordered my drink from the bartender, the man next to me recognized me. He said, "Hey, didn't I see you on the news the other day?" I said, "Oh, well, I don't know. Maybe?" He replied, "I live down in Lake Charles. You are the firefighter riding across the country, aren't you?" I smiled. He reached his hand out, he is a businessman, and said, "My name is Luke, it's great to meet you. It's pretty inspiring what you're doing." He slipped me a twenty-dollar bill for my drink. What just happened? It is pretty bizarre a stranger saying, did I see you on the news? And they remember the story.

Sitting out front, I notice a homeless guy on the corner. I approach him and asks if he is hungry. He pets Rocky, smiles, and shows me his sign. It reads "I'm deaf, alone and hungry." I hold up my hands in the eating motion, he nods, and I try to elaborate with movements to come get some food with me. It's hot outside, the city is loud, dirty, and muggy, and even in this humid heat, he is covered from head to toe in ripped, smelly clothing, and shrugged over in a wool blanket. My heart screams for these lost souls, suffering and withering away.

I thought I was hopeless in my suffering; now I stand back and look at him. A lady walks by, sees me trying to communicate with this man. She stops, in a classy, black business skirt, with her white dress shirt tucked in and her light chestnut hair wrapped in a bun, with an alligator designer purse hanging over her left shoulder. She peers down at the man's sign, and asks me what I am trying to say. I tell her, "I want to know if he wants to have lunch with me, right over here." I point to the restaurant. She tilts her head, and smiles. She starts doing sign language to the man. He looks down, at his clothes, and signs back to her, "They won't let me over there." I tell her to sign back to him, "Yes, they will. I got you, brother, come on." He is hesitant. I stick my hand out, I help him up, and give him a hug. He signs to her, and the lady says he wants to know my name. "I'm Kevin."

Rocky, the man, and I sit at one of the outdoor tables. We eat lunch together, have a cold drink in the heat. He holds his hands in a praying gesture, and it looks like his lips are saying thank you. I smile, but deep down, I want to cry. What a hard life this man has. I wish I could do more, but just as my father did with me, I sit there with him. And most of the time, that is all we need. Someone to just be there with us.

We just sat there, silently; he seemed to be happy, at least for this short moment together. As I may have helped him, he helped me too. I was sad about my dad leaving, and the journey coming to an end soon. So, we just sat there with each other, and he was there for me too. I remember thinking, funny how that worked out.

My father was worried that I might not get any support for the rest of the ride, being out of the west and heavy wildfire part of the country. I assured him everything works out. When you pour out love to the world, watch it flood back in.

After lunch, I see I have a voicemail on my phone.

"Hey, Kevin—my name is Doug Currie, I'm the forest AFMO in the Kisatchie down here in Louisiana. I'm sitting down here with eight of my folks and we are trying to figure out what kind of help you need tomorrow to get out of this great state and to unfortunately Mississippi. So, give me a holler back and let's figure out what you need and how we can help you accomplish that. This number works, thanks for what you're doing and talk to you soon."

Wow. The string of miracles from Wildland Firefighters that has strung across the entire country has been humbling; what remarkable, amazing humans. I give him a call back, and share some stories, laughs, and tell him what would help me the most. Like always that is someone watching Rocky for the day, so I can hammer out some bigger miles, in my attempt to make it home for Christmas. Doug is enthusiastic to help, as are his folks. I couldn't believe they even knew who I was; so many angels I didn't even know about were making calls and aligning the people together for me. I can't stress enough my gratitude; what a community I am lucky enough to be a part of.

I get off the phone with Doug; he tells me he's going to make a few calls, sit back and relax and we will have someone coming to get Rocky tomorrow morning. Magic. I hop in the shower, and when I get out, only a few minutes after talking with Doug, I have a new voicemail.

"Hey, Kevin—this is Mike, the helicopter manager up here on the Kisatchie. First off, great voicemail, man, and I definitely think what you're doing is for a great cause, and I appreciate what you're doing.

Anyways, Doug passed along your number and said you were looking for some help with your partner in crime, your four-legged friend, your pup. Give me a call back on how I can help and what you need from me."

The next day, after a well-needed rest and ice on my legs, Mike drove a few hours to pick Rocky up, we had some coffee together and a nice conversation. He had to get going, and I had to start riding again. What a guy, I can't believe how far he drove to help, I sort of feel guilty about it, but very grateful.

A women named Stacee Sadler has followed my story from the beginning and was the magic behind the scenes down here in the Southeast that I didn't know was taking place. She was the one who coordinated with everyone in Louisiana, Alabama, and Mississippi. This is what Stacee sent me:

"I don't remember when I first heard about Kevin's ride across the country. I know it was from one of many Wildlands Firefighter accounts I follow on Instagram, but I couldn't tell you which one. I read about his mission to raise awareness of mental health while also raising money for the Wildland Firefighter Foundation and I found it inspiring. I am a wildland firefighter and knew what Kevin was doing was going to mean so much to our community. I really wanted to assist him in whatever small way I could. So, when I checked out his route and saw that it would pass near where I live, I reached out to offer my support as he came through the area. He let me know the most significant help would be for someone to watch his dog, Rocky, for a couple of days as he came out of New Orleans and across Mississippi and Alabama. This would allow him to get some bigger mileage days in as he was trying to complete the ride before Christmas. I told him I would try. I put the word out and it was awesome to see the positive responses I got back. Folks were eager to extend their support. Since I didn't know anyone in Louisiana, I called my friend Jason Miller and let him in on what Kevin needed. Jason was the AFMO on the Oakmulgee Ranger District in Alabama, and I knew he had a lot of contacts. He got in touch with the Chief 2 on the Kisatchie National Forest in Louisiana, Doug Currie. Doug then sent word out to the folks on his forest to see if anyone would be able to help. Michael Lewton, a firefighter there, volunteered. At that point Michael and I got into contact and worked out a plan to keep Rocky for the next couple of days. Michael would go to New Orleans to meet up with Kevin, pick Rocky up, and take him for the night. The next day we would meet near Biloxi, Mississippi, where I would take Rocky home with me. The day after, I would pass him along to the next link in the chain; some Florida Forest Service folks Kevin had previously made arrangements with. The plan went really well. I was even able to meet up with Kevin along his route so he could give Rocky some love and grab a few things he needed from Rocky's trailer. Rocky and I had so much fun together, and I was proud we were able to give Kevin an assist as he rode over 200 miles within those few days. About a week later I watched a video of Kevin finishing his ride in St. Augustine. He had made it."

***

I blasted out of Louisiana, then crossed Mississippi in less than twenty-four hours. Stacee surprised me on the side of the road to briefly see my little buddy, Rocky. The roads were flat, the forest and swamps were thick with trees and life, and there were bridges everywhere. I got chased by a few more dogs and that air horn saved the day. I was shocked by the poverty throughout the south; I passed by a property that had five trailers. One more beat up than the last and only one suitable for living, it appeared like they trashed one and then just got a new one and continued. Trash, old cars, weird things lined some of the swampy back roads; some areas looked like abandoned communities, but they were not.

Gavin called me, all the way back from Pine Valley, California. He admired the distance I covered, the journey, and got me a motel for the night. We have had some nice talks on my long cycling days. We laughed as we reminisced about him taking my 500-mile celebration picture almost 3,000 miles ago.

Some dude on a moped tried to race me, he didn't stand a chance and I never saw him again.

I witnessed an immaculate sunset as I approached Dauphin Island, egrets and herons fishing on the coastline and my bike cable snapped. I had to go up and over the bridge to the island stuck in a pretty high gear. It was difficult. I was fifty miles from a bike shop, but the sunset was too perfect to worry about that tonight. The next morning, I caught the ferry off the island and was dazzled by the soft, sandy beaches, following the coastline, flat roads and palm trees. I had to ride hard, being stuck in a high gear, which was getting me down the road pretty quickly.

I got to Pensacola, Florida where the first Catholic Mass was celebrated on August 15th, 1559. It was truly a speechless moment hitting Florida, my last state and a simple hop, skip, and a jump to St. Augustine.

I went to the bike shop to get my cable fixed; they admired my journey on the Southern Tier and did it for free. I did a quick interview with ABC Channel 3, then had a great second podcast with Brandon for Anchorpoint dubbed "An Epic Ride, Part 2." I was so grateful for Brandon giving me this platform to talk about my journey, my struggles with mental health and spread my message to other firefighters. Speaking with him for hours about my mental illness, the ride, healing, and helping others was so therapeutic for me. I am very grateful for his friendship and listening ears.

The next day, I met up with Joe, a Forest Service PIO, who was helping with Rocky for the next stretch. Joe got the *Pensacola News Journal* out for another interview, and they took some rad pictures of me riding. Joe watched Rocky for the next few days; he even took Rocky on the Wildland Firefighter Pack Test with him. Which is three miles, forty-five-pound pack, in forty-five minutes, so I reckon Rocky is now an honorary firefighter. Joe and I had a nice lunch together, and he asked, "When will you finish?" And it was wild, unreal with these words coming out of my mouth: "Wow, this weekend, Joe."

I had never been so grateful in my entire life; so many strangers and friends were there for me along this journey. I was so afraid, ashamed, and embarrassed to talk about my mental illness and thought people would judge and look down on me. It was the complete opposite;

people listened and helped me. A childhood friend, Colby, got me a hotel in St. Augustine, right on the beach, so I could relax a couple days after I finished. He sent me some money along the way, donated to the Wildland Firefighter Foundation and was just an incredible support and after years of not being close, we became homies again.

One of my best friends, Junior, listened to me ramble for an hour or two every other day, it seemed, of my journey. I was so lucky to have a friend like him; he knew I needed someone, and he was there, every step of the way. I hope I can be there for him one day; he will never know how much that meant to me, him listening and talking to me this whole journey.

Another best friend, Josh, one of the two people I asked for a gun when I was in a dark place, made a generous donation to the foundation and talked to me for hours on my long days as well. I was so grateful for the people that helped me through my struggle and got to witness the brightness at the other end. It was crazy for me to think, two months ago, it seemed like a world away but Colby and Josh heard me on the phone on my darkest of hours. And, now I was calling them, happy as could be, telling them I almost finished. What a fucking trip.

In a crossroads gas station, in Cottondale, Florida, I sit on the side eating nasty pizza and ice cream. In amazement, I hear someone say my name. I look over, and my friends Daniela and Simon, on the tandem bike, are pulling up. I haven't seen them since Texas and only briefly on a hillside. It is such a cool reunion. We chat for a bit, ride for a bit, and then plan to meet a few hundred miles down the road in St. Augustine to celebrate.

I blasted the next three days, back-to-back-to-back hundred-mile days. I wanted to finish strong and was in the best shape of my life. I dropped a powerful 118.4-mile day into Gainesville, Florida. It was crazy looking at my speedometer and it was reading 3,410 miles, holy cow.

Ludie met me at the hotel in Gainesville. Tom and his family on their way to the beach delivered Rocky back to me. Ludie was also a Forest Service POI and had set up the local news to do an interview. I was incredibly grateful for the Florida Forest Service bumping Rocky along the entire state until Gainesville. Such sweet, honorable folks.

It was sixty miles from Gainesville to Palatka, and after Palatka was only thirty miles to St. Augustine. Two easy days left. I was sure to soak in the moment, it was too sweet to taste anything other than to savor right where I was.

Rocky and I ate ice cream all day, stopped at a little festival on the side of the road and both had some giant ribs. I spoiled him after not seeing him for a while. He licked barbecue sauce off my face, and I just kissed him a thousand times, he is such a great dog. I wonder if he knows how far we traveled. He made countless new friends and saw more of the country than most humans. You ever heard of someone pulling their dog across the entire country?

We crossed the Saint Johns River as the sun set and full moon rose. It was our last night, and after dominating some huge miles to finish and get home for Christmas, I was pooped. We cuddled on the bed and watched part of a movie as I fell asleep almost immediately. Tomorrow was going to be one of the best days of my life, one of my greatest accomplishments on so many levels, and it had meaning greater than myself. I wanted to sleep well and be refreshed in the morning for our last little adventure on the Southern Tier.

It was bittersweet knowing tomorrow was the last day, and we were surrounded by palm trees once again. From the Pacific to the Atlantic Ocean, what a long bike ride. Feels like just yesterday, Rocky was chasing seagulls in Santa Monica.

"You must be ready to burn yourself in your own flame; how could you rise anew if you have not first become ashes?"

-Friedrich Nietzsche

CHAPTER 15

All Tied In

I risked every penny I had...to set off on this challenge of riding my bicycle across the entire country. I risked all I had to hopefully find peace and clarity once again. After a long and painful year of feeling hopeless, I risked it all to find that feeling of hope once again, which I gratefully found. I risked it all because I was done living in hell, through depression and my panic disorder; I had to reach out of my comfort zone to battle my demons, one on one, and overcome them. I risked it all, because I stared death in the face, and this was my last shot to find self-love once again. I strongly believe that if I didn't go on this journey, I would've eventually ended my life.

Once I took off on this journey, there was no turning back. I left Salt Lake City on a mission, a mission that I set three major goals for myself to accomplish. To better myself, through finding clarity and peace in my mind, healing, and letting go; also, to raise money for the Wildland Firefighter Foundation; and lastly to raise awareness about mental health. I can now look back and smile, knowing I accomplished all three of those goals. I was a new person, a better person. I was lost and now I was found; I was hopeless and now I am beyond full of hope. I am a dreamer again, motivated again and in love with life and loving who I am again. I found peace, and I put my demons to rest.

The journey flashes in front of my eyes as I lace up my shoes for my last push, the final twenty-eight miles to St. Augustine and seeing the Atlantic Ocean. Goosebumps flow up my arms, a big smile lies on my face, my eyes twinkle as the morning sun greets them. It feels surreal, like a dream; pinch me, how am I here? I can't remember the last time I felt this excited and this proud; only a far journey like this one truly puts you into a state of awe and appreciation. Accomplishing such a huge feat, all human powered, is one of true bliss.

At the beginning I felt like a glass ball, tumbling down into the abyss. Now I realize, I was not made of glass, I was a boulder, a hardened rock. I was born on the mountain, the mountain wasn't a part of me, I was the mountain. Its highs and lows, I have felt it all, and today I sit up high. However, I know, one day, I will fall again. How far will I roll? Will I tumble all the way into the valley again? I don't know. What I do know is now I am strong, I am not afraid of going back down there; I know and understand what down there feels like. And I've learned that I can climb back up, more importantly, I know how to climb back up. The views are too grand and magical from up here to stay down there for too long ever again. I will cherish this high, this happiness, and hold onto it for as long as I can.

It is okay to not be okay. It's okay to speak about mental illness and health. It is okay to be depressed; it is okay to ask for help. It is okay to be you. Embrace your feelings.

A couple months ago I almost killed myself. I was so sick of suffering with my panic disorder and depression, and I didn't want to live anymore. In the blink of an eye, I decided to ride my bicycle 3,500 miles across the country. To sit with my emotions and my feelings and learn how to cope with them without any escape or crutch. To reteach my brain. And this bike ride across the country saved my life and got me back where I wanted to be. I want to remind people, no matter how dark, or how scary, or how lonely, or how depressed, or how much you want it to end...No matter the hell you are going through, YOU CAN OVERCOME IT! I almost killed myself and now I'm extremely grateful for EVERY. MOMENT. I. HAVE. No matter what adversity you go through, you can become better...Emotionally, physically, spiritually, however you want to get better, you can. And I hope that you never give up. Always believe in yourself and NEVER EVER GIVE UP. I almost gave up and now I'm happy as ever because I fought for it, and I didn't give up. I love you!

I hope you know you have so much power within you. I wish I could shake you, and you could feel the power I have discovered, and I could give you just a piece of it, so you would know, you can overcome anything, and everything will be all right. You have it all within you, the power to give up or the power to giddy up and overcome.

Remember, it IS the small things.

This achievement would not feel this way if I had not suffered and sacrificed. Nothing great comes to you without suffering. I needed to feel that pain, in order for me to understand what this joy truly is.

Forgive yourself.

Routine is critical. A cluttered mind is a cluttered life. Get things done, don't let things build up. Be a go-getter, a goal setter, a dream chaser and a dream catcher, a selfless spirit; be a kind, compassionate, and hardworking soul.

Attitude is everything.

Hold yourself accountable. Be a good human. Stand up for what is right.

Ask yourself, when is the last time you did something that you will remember for the rest of your life?

Ask yourself. When is the last time I did something for someone else that they will remember for the rest of theirs?

Are you living the life you could be living? What are you waiting for? Go out there and fucking LIVE!

I thought I was weak.

I am strong.

I thought I was fragile.

I am unbreakable.

I thought I wasn't good enough.

I am. I am me, and that is who I want to be. Happy or sad, I am me. I love me.

I thought I was a quitter.

I am a warrior that will never use that word again.

I thought I was dying.

I am alive, I am full of energy and life.

I thought I didn't want to see tomorrow.

I am the moment.

I thought this was it.

I am optimism. I am positivity. I am inspired. This is only the beginning.

I thought it couldn't get better.

I am better.

I thought I was all alone.

I am one of many who have mentally suffered. We are not alone.

I thought I couldn't go on.

I am the only one who can get myself to go on and go on I have.

I thought I was powerless.

I am POWERFUL.

I thought a lot of things, and they were not real. They were only a perception that I had. They were not my reality, just how I perceived my reality was. When I changed my perception, I saw a new reality. The reality is, no matter what you go through in life, if you fight back, you can and you will get better and overcome any obstacle that stands in your way. The reality is you have the power to overcome anything and the strength to adapt to any situation. You are a superhero, and I hope you see that.

I strived in this story to show you that you can come from rock bottom and accomplish things way past what you could've ever imagined. What would you do next, if you knew you couldn't fail?

Consistency is KEY.

Anything is possible.

***

As I woke up that morning in Palatka, Florida on the Saint Johns River, I stuck to our morning routine. Playing fetch with Rocky and a cup of coffee. I felt amazing, as a misting of cooling rain came down from the cloudy morning skies. There was nothing that could take this feeling out of my heart and soul. I was so darn happy, and my adrenaline was off the charts and ready to ride these last twenty-eight miles with all my power and ability.

Brandon from the Anchorpoint Podcast had reached out to the St. Augustine Fire Department. He got in touch with a dispatcher named Abby. Abby and I spoke the day before I would finish in St. Augustine. She told me she was going to try to get their two local fire engines to the finish line to cheer me on. However, they could be out on calls and not available. I had no idea what was going to happen when I arrived, but I shot her a text and said I will shoot to be in downtown St. Augustine at noon.

Sean Gallagher, the Forest Service Deputy Chief, whom I spoke with way back in California, was on his way to meet me at the hotel and ride the last twenty-eight miles with me. He also had one of his wildland brush fire engines coming to meet us for the last few miles to escort us to the finish line.

One of my best childhood friends, Greg Prompovitch, was driving up with his wife to celebrate at the finish line and take some professional photos.

My two friends on the tandem bike were also finishing today. Daniela and Simon were planning on meeting at the finish line so we could share that moment and camp together that night on the beach and share stories around a campfire.

Also, my dad's friend Jeff Tabor and his son were driving down from Jacksonville to witness my completion of the Southern Tier.

Sean showed up right on time. He looked spiffy in his red, white, and blue cycling spandex and on a very nice, lift-it-with-a-finger bicycle. I warned him about my speed, with Rocky and the trailer, and offered him to spin it around the parking lot. He laughed and was shocked that I towed this thing all the way from San Francisco. We shook hands, and just like that, we were off.

My spirits were high, and I pedaled like I never had before this last day. Fierce, swift, and I stood up nearly the entirety of the last twenty-eight miles. Sean rode tightly, behind me, as we cranked down the decently trafficked Route 207, a straight shot to St. Augustine. This moment is so beautiful, it's so hard to describe, the last push of a 3,500-mile journey. I'm so alive, breathing in the moment and pedaling with so much power. I've never pulled Rocky with this much strength, like the 150 pounds behind me evaporated; it feels as though I am weightless; a man on a mission, I can feel the finish line. With my shirt off, my hat tucked tight, my curly hair waving in the wind, sweat dripping off me, and laughter spontaneously hitting me, I think about how special this moment is.

With a mile left, the Forest Service Engine comes to my side and hands me an American flag. I cruise ahead. Sean and I now have the Forest Service Engine escorting us from behind with their lights on. We are getting closer, Sean hollers up with a great, big smile on his face, "Kevin, this is it, brother, it's right up there."

I can't stop smiling, my heart pounding in joy and excitement. I proudly raise that American flag high up and wave it back and forth. There are two big, structure fire trucks with their lights on, a police car with his lights on, an ambulance too. A half dozen firefighters holding up signs, "WAY TO GO, KEVIN," "3,500 MILES." The red lights are flashing behind as I ride the last hundred yards; everyone downtown is wondering what is going on.

With policeman, firefighters, EMTs and a couple dozen people cheering loudly, I barrel through the finish line, proudly waving this American flag and smiling. I pull over, pop Rocky out of his trailer and give him a big kiss, we did it, buddy! He runs around, meeting all his new friends. Abby gives me a big hug, and surprises me with some champagne. I shake everyone's hand, one by one, and thank them so much for being there, and thank Abby for coordinating such a special moment. Random people come from the sidewalks to congratulate me and shake my hand. I take some pictures with Sean, Matt Dedmon, and Mike Bowman, the Wildland Firefighting folks, and express my gratitude. I do the same with the St. Augustine first responders.

I never in a million years expected this journey to end in such a special way.

Just like I said in my first news interview, that I was going to finish on my mother's birthday. Today, the day I accomplished my goal, December 19th, coincidentally was it.

I soak in the moment; it is such an amazing one.

I give a big hug to my tandem-riding friends and congratulate them for their huge accomplishment as well. I thank everyone for coming out and making this such a magical ending to a fairytale of a story.

Daniela, Simon, and I and my childhood friend Greg and his wife cruised down to the beach. I wanted to bring this journey full circle; Rocky and I camped the first night, so I wanted to camp the last one too. We got to the beach, ripped off our shirts, and sprinted down and dove into the waves and into the Atlantic Ocean. Rocky came rushing in behind us, he got beat down by the waves; I didn't think he was going to follow me. But the trusty, loyal best friend he is, as he always does, he stuck by my side.

We sat on the beach for an hour or so. In awe of the long ride from the Pacific and now we are swimming in the Atlantic, all on a bicycle.

We reminisced around the warm fire, under a blanket of stars as the ocean crashed sweet melodies behind us. We laughed through the night.

Thirty-five hundred miles pedaling to peace, 3,500 miles rising Above the Ashes, 3,500 miles to rediscover joy, 3,500 miles to free myself from my battle with mental illness.

I am a champion in my own mind.

Those 3,500 miles saved my life.

Afterword

By Burk Minor

Executive Director - Wildland Firefighter Foundation

     Kevin's journey is a road that many first responders find themselves stuck on, just trudging along like the little soldiers that they train proudly to be. Train as you fight, fight as you train, BE MENTALLY TOUGH. You got this! Those of you who have done the job, you know. This mental health road does not decipher who travels it. It does not care how you got there or why. The road chuckles and whispers in your ear like the serpent talking to Eve, "If you tell them that you are not okay, they will think that you are weak. Who cares that you jump out of an airplane; so what you slide down a rope from a helicopter; big deal you're a Hotshot; look at mister tough guy over there carrying all those hose packs. You all know that as soon as fire season is over, you're going to get laid off until they need you again, and to top it off, nobody cares!" These are just a few visual slides or the repetitive voices that some cannot turn off or put out of their head. Perception is Reality. Some people are too scared and/or too proud to ask for help, choosing to face and fight their demons head-on, alone, battling it out every minute of every day until they can't any longer. Trudging along the road to nowhere until they have reached a dead end. Can't turn left, can't turn right, can't turn back, and definitely can't continue to move forward. They have reached the end of the road, their journey and story end here. No pause for thought, it's just done.

Those left behind doing the "would've, could've, should've." In his or her state of mind, Perception is Reality. Then there are folks like Kevin. Trudging along that same road, turning left turning right, turning back and moving forward all the while fighting and battling it out with the demons and the voices in their heads. They know that out there is peace and comfort for their mind, body, and soul, yet they just have to do what they need to do in or out of the box, with or without help in order to get there and find it. They are like the Little Engine That Could.

When I listened to Kevin's voicemail, and then we had a conversation; at first, I didn't know what to make of it but I knew that I was going to support him, not for the benefit of the fundraiser but in support of Kevin. Riding your bike with your dog across America if that's what it takes to help you find where the gaps are in your life and to get rid of the clutter in your brain, more power to you brother; get on it and we will support you and your journey all the way. The more I watched Kevin through this journey, his hair went from Hippy mode to shaved and respectful. I have no doubt this was not only from his own healing but also from the lives that touched him on his journey. At the end of Kevin's ride, I was beside myself to see other full-grown men who approached him and thanked him for having the courage to speak out, as it gave them the courage to speak out and admit that they were suffering too. Here at the Wildland Firefighter Foundation, we listen to many stories from those who are suffering or have suffered the trials and tribulations of mental trauma, including but not limited to, addiction, the stresses of daily life, issues that we, nor you could ever imagine a person going through, and of course, grief. The Wildland Firefighter Foundation is the brainchild of my mother, Vicki Minor. In 1994, the idea of the foundation was born and the Wildland Firefighter Foundation formed officially in 1999. Back then, the focus of the foundation was "to provide immediate financial and crisis assistance to families of fallen and injured wildland firefighters. To recognize and honor fallen wildland firefighters past, present, and future. To immediately respond to situations that involve the loss or injury of a wildland firefighter and this one right here, an organization adaptive to an ever-changing environment." Back then the crisis assistance pretty much focused mainly on grief and bereavement for family members and other survivors. I don't think at the time mental illness or trauma was recognized in the wildland fire community or in any of the fire/first responder communities, for that matter, and if it was, it wasn't talked about. Firefighters are the toughest of the tough, both physically and mentally you don't dare ask for help, you fix it yourself, this is where a lot of the addictive habits begin; and/or suffer alone. In the minds of most, the belief is that if you ask for help, you still lose, as now everyone knows that you are the weak link and are not tough like them. Mental Health at times is a loose situation. You are damned if you do and damned if you don't. Did you know that most deaths to wildland firefighters don't occur on the fire ground? Our current stats [1]show from 2019 to present time there were 216 deaths. Of those, thirty were Suicide Completions. That is

---

[1] Our statistics may differ from other Firefighter Fatality databases. We track both Line, Active and Non Line of Duty deaths of wildland firefighters and those who have died while in the direct suppression of wildland fire. The database is fluid as we update when we receive notification and information for a death or fatality, from a past or current incident.

thirty too many. As far as we know, only one Suicide Completion was deemed a Line of Duty Death as the firefighter asked for help after a traumatizing incident, the agency recognized, accepted, and provided treatment to the firefighter; however, the mental trauma was too much for the firefighter to bear. Firefighters need to start documenting your mental injuries as you do your physical injuries. It's not about, excuse the morbidity here, benefits and making sure that your family is taken care of should you ever suffer a traumatic event that can put you on that dead end road; it's about getting help when you need it most. Let's make a deal; if you are afraid to ask for help fearing repercussion (or whatever your perception of the outcome of your request for help might be), just give us a call, if not us, CALL SOMEBODY! Spread the word! Don't hesitate to pick up the phone or shoot us an email for your buddy if your buddy won't or can't. Simply put, we can't provide assistance or guidance if we don't know you or someone else has a need. No matter what the need might be, reach out to us, let us know what's going on and if we can't help, we will find someone who can. As the intricate pieces of the wildland fire community continuously evolve, you can count on one thing; we will always have your back.

You can contact us in the following ways:

Call us at (208) 336 2996

Email us at info@wffoundation.org

For more information about who we are and what we do, go to our website: wffoundation.org. If you are looking for information or are in need of assistance in dealing with a crisis and can't quite yet make a call, click the Resources/Self Help tab. You can also send us a message or email through the website, just click on the contact tab. Kevin, may you and those who are reading my words continue to fight as you rise above the ashes.

Burk

Acknowledgments

I would like to first thank my mother, Kathleen, for the incredible gift of life. For watching over me and being the best mother those nine months in the womb, and the thirty-five years since. You're such a strong and brave woman.

Thank you to my father, for always believing in me, pushing me to be better and being such a very special part of this journey. You definitely are the father to me that you never had.

Thank you to my little brother, John, for never giving up on me. I put him through hell as a child, and I just hope you know I'm always here for you, buddy! Can't wait for your wedding. Ouia Douia

Thank you to the countless donors who made my fundraising efforts a very successful endeavor. Thank you so much for your support!

My dear friend Marcus Blaha that has been the epitome of a best friend for 20 years, thank you.

I can't thank enough, the beautiful people, firefighters, and all the beautiful humans who assisted me, in so many ways along my journey. So grateful to you all. Ya'll helped me heal more than you will ever know.

Thank you to the Wildland Firefighter Foundation. Who they are, what they represent, and what they do. It is with great honor that I can donate some of the profits from this book back to you.

And, to my dearest little rugrat, my sweet boy, Rocky. Truly, man's best friend.

God Bless America.

I love you all.

9ab2798d-31f3-4035-83e3-0e446f8902f4R01